The Stupid History Book

Volume One

Keb Pound

DEDICATION

I would like to dedicate this book to my Parents, who have always
supported me in anything that I have ever wanted to do.

ACKNOWLEDGMENTS

I am honored to acknowledge the individuals who have played a significant role in the completion of this book.

Firstly, I would like to express my gratitude to my family & close friends for their support, encouragement, and unwavering ability to put up with my nonsense. Their love and belief in me throughout the years is the one thing that has kept me going even during the most challenging moments.

I also want to extend my heartfelt thanks to my podcast family, who provided invaluable feedback and guidance (whether I asked for it or not) that helped shape this work.

Finally, I express my appreciation to the readers and everyone who has listened to the podcast for investing their time in learning about Stupid History.

Hello and welcome to The Stupid History Book.

I'm the author, Keb Pound.

Today we're talking about…

1 BLENDERS

Blenders are one of the most used appliances in the modern-day kitchen. They are used for a variety of purposes, from blending fruits and vegetables to make smoothies to grinding coffee beans for that perfect cup of coffee. However, the history of blenders dates to more than a century ago.

The first blender was invented in 1922 by Stephen Poplawski, a Polish American inventor. Poplawski was a bartender in Wisconsin, and he invented the blender to make it easier to mix drinks. He realized that by blending the ingredients, he could make drinks that were smoother and had a better texture.

Poplawski's original blender was called the "drink mixer" and was designed to be used in bars and restaurants. It consisted of a spinning blade at the bottom of a tall container, which could be used to mix drinks, chop ice, and blend fruit.

In the years that followed, blenders became increasingly popular in households as well. In 1937, the first blender designed for home use was introduced by the Hamilton Beach Company. This blender was called the "Miracle Mixer" and had a glass container with a detachable blade assembly.

During World War II, blenders were used by the military to blend food for soldiers. After the war, blenders became even more popular, and new features and designs were introduced. In 1949, the Oster company introduced the "Osterizer," which was the first blender to have a rotating blade inside a glass container. The Osterizer quickly became the most popular blender on the market and remained so for several decades.

In the 1950s, blenders became a symbol of the American dream and were featured in many advertisements. They were seen as a modern and convenient appliance that every household should have. During this time, blenders became more powerful, with higher wattage motors and more advanced blade designs.

In the 1960s and 1970s, blenders continued to evolve, with new features such as pulse control and variable speeds. These features allowed users to have more control over the blending process, making it easier to achieve the desired texture for different types of food.

In the 1980s, blenders became more specialized, with models designed for specific uses such as making smoothies or crushing ice. The popularity of smoothies helped to drive the demand for more powerful and versatile blenders.

In the 1990s and 2000s, blenders continued to evolve, with new features such as digital displays and pre-programmed settings. These features made it easier to use blenders and allowed for more precise control over the blending process.

Today, blenders come in a wide range of sizes, shapes, and styles, and there is a blender to suit every need and budget. From personal blenders for single servings to high-performance blenders for commercial use, blenders continue to be an essential appliance in kitchens around the world.

2 BALLOONS

Balloons have been used for centuries for various purposes such as transportation, entertainment, and scientific experiments. The history of balloons dates to ancient times when people first discovered the principles of buoyancy and started using lighter-than-air objects to achieve flight.

The first recorded instance of balloons being used for flight dates to the 3rd century BC in China. It is believed that the Chinese used hot air balloons made of paper or silk, which were filled with hot air from a fire source. These balloons were used for military signaling and communication purposes, but they were not capable of carrying humans or cargo.

It wasn't until the late 18th century that the first manned balloon flight took place. On November 21, 1783, two French brothers, Joseph and Etienne Montgolfier, launched a hot air balloon from the Palace of Versailles. The balloon, which was made of paper and cloth and filled with hot air, carried two passengers - Jean-Francois Pilatre de Rozier and Francois Laurent - to a height of 5.5 miles before landing safely. This historic flight marked the beginning of the modern era of ballooning.

Following the success of the Montgolfier brothers, several other pioneers took to the skies in balloons. In 1784, Jean-Pierre Blanchard and John Jeffries became the first people to cross the English Channel in a balloon. Two years later, Andre-Jacques Garnerin became the first person to make a parachute descent from a balloon.

In the early 19th century, hydrogen gas balloons became popular, as they could carry heavier payloads and stay aloft for longer periods of time than hot air balloons. In 1835, Frenchman Jules Duruof made the first successful long-distance balloon flight, traveling from Paris to Germany in 18 hours.

Throughout the 19th and early 20th centuries, balloons were used for a variety of purposes, including scientific research, military reconnaissance, and exploration. During World War I, both the Allies and the Central Powers used observation balloons for reconnaissance purposes. In World War II, balloons were used as a form of psychological warfare, with the Japanese launching thousands of balloons carrying incendiary and explosive devices to the west coast of the United States.

In the post-World War II era, balloons continued to be used for scientific research and exploration. In 1960, American pilot Joseph Kittinger made the highest-ever balloon ascent, reaching a height of 102,800 feet. In 1986, the first balloon circumnavigation of the earth was completed by Richard Branson and Per Lindstrand.

Today, balloons are used primarily for entertainment purposes, such as balloon races, festivals, and hot air balloon rides. Ballooning has become a popular hobby and sport, with enthusiasts participating in events such as balloon races and long-distance balloon flights.

3 AIRBAGS

Airbags have become a standard safety feature in most modern automobiles, but the concept of a safety cushion that deploys during a collision has been around for over a century.

The idea of using an air-filled cushion as a safety feature can be traced back to the early 1900s. John W. Hetrick, an engineer from the United States, came up with the idea of an air-filled cushion that could protect people during a car crash. Hetrick came up with the idea while driving his own vehicle and almost collided with a tree. He thought that if he could create a cushion that could absorb the impact of the crash, it could save lives.

Hetrick patented his idea in 1951, but it wasn't until the 1970s that airbags began to be developed and tested in earnest. In 1971, General Motors introduced the first experimental airbag system, which was installed in a fleet of Chevrolet Impalas. These systems used sensors to detect the sudden deceleration of the vehicle and deployed the airbags in a fraction of a second.

Over the next decade, several other manufacturers, including Ford and Chrysler, developed their own airbag systems. However, these systems were expensive, bulky, and often unreliable. It wasn't until the mid-1980s that airbags began to be widely adopted in the automotive industry.

In 1984, the Mercedes-Benz S-Class became the first production car to feature a driver-side airbag as standard equipment. The same year, General Motors began offering airbags as an option on several of its models. By the end of the decade, most automakers had made airbags a standard feature on their vehicles.

Despite the widespread adoption of airbags, there were still issues that needed to be addressed. Early airbag systems were known to cause injuries, particularly to small children and elderly passengers. In some cases, the force of the airbag deploying could cause more harm than the crash itself.

To address these issues, manufacturers began developing more advanced airbag systems that could sense the size and position of the occupants in the vehicle. These systems would then adjust the force of the airbag deployment to minimize the risk of injury.

In the 1990s, the National Highway Traffic Safety Administration (NHTSA) began requiring all new passenger cars and light trucks to be equipped with both driver and passenger airbags. By the early 2000s, side airbags and curtain airbags had become standard equipment on many vehicles.

Today, airbags are an essential safety feature in most modern automobiles. In addition to the standard front airbags, many vehicles now feature side airbags, curtain airbags, and even knee airbags. These systems work together with other safety features, such as seat belts and electronic stability control, to help protect occupants in the event of a crash.

4 BARBEQUE GRILLS

Barbecue grills have become a staple of outdoor cooking in many cultures around the world. The history of the barbecue grill dates to the discovery of fire, but the modern grill as we know it today has come a long way since its inception.

The origin of the word "barbecue" is believed to be from the Taino language, spoken by indigenous people of the Caribbean islands. The Taino word "barbacoa" refers to a wooden platform that was used for cooking meat over an open fire. The Spanish explorers who arrived in the Caribbean in the 15th century adopted the word "barbacoa" and introduced it to the rest of the world.

In the early days of barbecue, cooking was done over open fires using crude grills made of wood and stones. As technology advanced, so did the design of the barbecue grill. In the late 1800s, the first portable grills were introduced, made of cast iron and fueled by charcoal.

One of the earliest and most well-known American barbecue grills is the Weber grill, invented by George Stephen Sr. in 1951. He was a metalworker who was inspired by the shape of a buoy and created a round grill with a lid, which allowed for better temperature control and the ability to smoke meat. The Weber grill became an instant hit and is still a popular choice for backyard barbecues today.

In the 1960s, gas grills were introduced as an alternative to charcoal grills. The first gas grill was invented by Don McGlaughlin, who owned a company called Chicago Combustion Corporation. The gas grill quickly became popular because of its convenience and ease of use.

The 1970s saw the introduction of electric grills, which allowed for indoor grilling and cooking in small spaces. Electric grills were also popular because they eliminated the need for fuel and were easy to clean.

In the 1990s, infrared grills were introduced, which used infrared technology to cook food more evenly and quickly. Infrared grills also produced less smoke and allowed for easier temperature control.

Today, there are many types of barbecue grills available on the market, including charcoal grills, gas grills, electric grills, and pellet grills. Pellet grills are a newer type of grill that uses wood pellets to fuel the fire and create a smoky flavor.

In addition to the evolution of the grill itself, barbecue culture has also undergone significant changes over the years. Barbecuing has become a popular social activity and is often associated with summertime gatherings, family reunions, and sporting events. In the United States, there are even regional barbecue styles, such as Memphis-style, Texas-style, and Kansas City-style barbecue.

5 CHOPSTICKS

Chopsticks are the most used utensils for eating in many parts of Asia, including China, Japan, Korea, and Vietnam. They are slender sticks that are used to pick up food and bring it to one's mouth. Chopsticks have a long history, with their origin dating back to ancient times.

The earliest known evidence of chopsticks dates to ancient China, around 1200 BC. The Chinese people used chopsticks for cooking and serving food, but they did not use them for eating until later. In the beginning, chopsticks were made from bamboo, which was plentiful in China, and were used to cook food over a fire.

Over time, chopsticks became more popular as a utensil for eating, and they began to be made from other materials, such as wood, ivory, and bone. The use of chopsticks also spread to other parts of Asia, such as Japan, Korea, and Vietnam.

In Japan, chopsticks were first used by the nobility and were made from lacquered wood. They were also used in religious ceremonies and were sacred objects. In the 17th century, chopsticks began to be mass-produced in Japan, and they became more widely available to the general population.

In Korea, chopsticks were traditionally made from metal or silver, and they were used in a different way than in other parts of Asia. Korean chopsticks are longer and flatter than Chinese or Japanese chopsticks, and they are used to scoop up food rather than to pick it up.

In Vietnam, chopsticks were also traditionally made from wood, and they were used in a similar way to Chinese chopsticks. However, in Vietnam, chopsticks were often used in combination with a spoon, with the chopsticks being used to pick up solid food and the spoon being used to eat soup and other liquid dishes.

In modern times, chopsticks have become a popular symbol of Asian culture and cuisine around the world. They are now commonly made from materials such as plastic and metal, and they are often decorated with colorful designs and patterns.

Despite their widespread use, chopsticks are not without controversy. Some people argue that the use of chopsticks is not hygienic, as they are not as easy to clean as other utensils. Others argue that the use of chopsticks is wasteful, as they are often disposable and contribute to environmental pollution.

6 CORNFLAKES

Cornflakes have become a staple breakfast cereal for millions of people worldwide. This simple, yet delicious food item has an interesting history that dates to the late 19th century.

The invention of cornflakes is credited to Dr. John Harvey Kellogg, who was a physician, health enthusiast, and the superintendent of the Battle Creek Sanitarium in Michigan. Dr. Kellogg believed that a healthy diet was essential for good health and sought to develop a food that would be easy to digest, nutritious, and most importantly, delicious.

In 1894, while experimenting with different types of grains, Dr. Kellogg accidentally left a pot of boiled wheat on the stove for too long. The wheat became stale and hard, but instead of throwing it away, he decided to pass it through a set of rollers. This process created flakes of wheat, which he then toasted and served to his patients.

The toasted wheat flakes were an instant hit with his patients and Dr. Kellogg realized that he had stumbled upon a new type of food that could be a healthy alternative to traditional breakfast options. He began experimenting with different grains and in 1898, he developed the first cornflakes.

Initially, the cornflakes were not well received, and Dr. Kellogg struggled to market them. It wasn't until his younger brother, Will Keith Kellogg, joined the Sanitarium and began helping him with the business that cornflakes became a household name.

In 1906, Will Keith Kellogg left the Sanitarium to start his own cereal company, the Kellogg Company, which is still in existence today. Will Keith

Kellogg was a savvy businessman and recognized the potential of cornflakes. He developed a marketing campaign that focused on the health benefits of cornflakes, and the cereal soon became popular across the United States.

As the popularity of cornflakes grew, other cereal companies began to develop their own versions of the cereal. One of the most notable was Post Cereals, which developed Grape-Nuts, a cereal that was similar in texture to cornflakes but was made from a blend of wheat and barley.

Today, cornflakes are sold in nearly every country in the world, and there are countless variations and flavors available. While they may not be as trendy or fashionable as some of the more recent breakfast trends, cornflakes remain a classic and beloved breakfast staple for millions of people.

7 FORKS

The fork is a utensil that is used to transfer food from a plate to the mouth. It has been around for centuries and has undergone numerous changes throughout its history.

The earliest known forks were used in ancient Egypt and were made from bronze. These forks were used to skewer meat while it was being cooked. However, they were not used for eating, as it was believed that fingers were the best utensil for that purpose. In fact, many cultures believed this, and it was not until the Middle Ages that forks began to be used for eating.

The first forks for eating were used in the Byzantine Empire in the 4th century. These forks were two-pronged and were used primarily for serving fruit and other delicacies. They were made from silver and were used only by the wealthy. The use of forks for eating was seen as a sign of refinement and sophistication, and it was not until several centuries later that they became more widespread.

In the 11th century, forks began to appear in Italy. These forks were like the ones used in the Byzantine Empire, but they had three or four prongs instead of two. They were still primarily used by the wealthy, but they became more common in the following centuries.

In the 16th century, forks became more widely used throughout Europe. They were still primarily used by the wealthy, but they began to appear in more households. However, the use of forks was still seen as controversial by some, and there were those who believed that they were an unnecessary extravagance. In fact, the writer Montaigne wrote in the 16th century that he had never seen a fork before he went to Italy, and that he saw it as a "marvelous luxury."

Despite this controversy, the use of forks continued to spread throughout Europe. By the 17th century, they had become a common household item in many parts of the continent. In England, however, forks were slower to catch on. They were not commonly used until the 18th century, and even then, they were seen as a luxury item.

One of the most significant changes in the history of forks came in the 19th century when the design of the fork was improved. In 1851, a man named Samuel W. Francis patented the first fork with a curved tine. This design made it easier to scoop up food and was a significant improvement over the straight-tined forks that had been used up until that point.

Another major change came with the introduction of stainless steel in the early 20th century. Stainless steel is durable and easy to clean, making it an ideal material for utensils. Today, most forks are made from stainless steel, and they come in a wide variety of designs and sizes.

In addition to the standard dinner fork, there are many other types of forks that are used for specific purposes. Salad forks, for example, have longer tines that make it easier to pick up lettuce and other leafy greens. Dessert forks are smaller and have narrower tines, making them ideal for eating cake and other sweets. There are also seafood forks, which have a narrow, pointed tine that is used for extracting meat from shellfish.

8 LEGOS

Lego is a Danish company that is renowned worldwide for its iconic and colorful building blocks. These blocks are known to be loved by people of all ages, and their success is credited to their flexibility and versatility, allowing people to build whatever they like. Lego's history dates to 1932, when Ole Kirk Christiansen, a carpenter, started a small company that made wooden toys.

In 1932, Ole Kirk Christiansen founded a small company in Billund, Denmark, called "Lego," which is derived from the Danish words "leg godt," which means "play well." The company originally produced wooden toys, such as pull-along ducks and trucks, and produced plastic toys, such as yo-yos and plastic blocks, before they found their niche in the plastic building block industry.

The company's first plastic block was produced in 1949, and it was made from cellulose acetate. These blocks were not the interlocking blocks we know today but were instead hollow, and the blocks were held together using wooden dowels. In 1953, the company began producing interlocking blocks that could be easily assembled and disassembled. These early interlocking blocks were also made from cellulose acetate.

In 1958, the modern Lego brick was born. It was made of a tougher plastic called acrylonitrile butadiene styrene (ABS), and it was designed to be more stable and versatile than its predecessors. The new brick design included a tube-like structure that allowed the blocks to lock together more securely, making them ideal for building larger structures. The new design also featured a more precise tolerance, which made the blocks more consistent in size and shape, further improving their interlocking ability.

The new Lego brick design was an instant success, and it quickly became the company's flagship product. Over the years, Lego has continued to innovate and improve upon its brick design, introducing new colors, sizes, and shapes, as well as adding themed sets and licensed products. In 1978, Lego introduced its first licensed product line, "Star Wars," which has been one of its most successful product lines to date.

In addition to its product line, Lego has also been successful in creating a strong brand image. The company has an instantly recognizable logo and has built a reputation for quality and creativity. Lego's commitment to innovation and creativity has also helped the company stay relevant, with new product releases and marketing campaigns that appeal to a wide audience.

Over the years, Lego has become an icon of pop culture, and it has been featured in movies, television shows, and video games. The company's most significant pop culture impact has been in the world of animation, with its line of Lego movies and television shows. The Lego Movie, released in 2014, was a massive success, grossing over $469 million worldwide. The movie spawned several sequels, including The Lego Batman Movie and The Lego Ninjago Movie.

The company has also released several video games, such as Lego Star Wars and Lego Marvel Superheroes, which have been popular among gamers of all ages. In addition to its impact on pop culture, Lego has also had a significant impact on education, with the company partnering with schools and educators to create programs that teach children about science, technology, engineering, and mathematics (STEM) through play.

9 PLAY-DOH

Play-Doh is one of the most beloved children's toys of all time, a brightly colored, malleable substance that can be molded and shaped into countless forms. Since its inception in the 1930s, Play-Doh has become a staple of playtime for generations of children around the world, inspiring creativity and imagination in millions of young minds.

The history of Play-Doh began in the 1930s, when a man named Noah McVicker was trying to create a wallpaper cleaner. McVicker was working for a soap company called Kutol Products, which was struggling to stay afloat during the Great Depression. To save the company, McVicker and his team began experimenting with different formulas for cleaning products.

One of the formulas they came up with was a soft, pliable substance made from flour, water, salt, boric acid, and mineral oil. This substance was designed to be used as a cleaning agent, but McVicker soon realized that it had other uses as well. Children who saw the substance in the factory began playing with it, molding it into different shapes and objects.

Realizing that they had stumbled upon something special, McVicker and Kutol Products decided to market the substance as a children's toy. They renamed it "Kutol's Rainbow Modeling Compound" and began selling it in local stores. However, the product did not sell well, and Kutol Products was on the verge of bankruptcy once again.

In 1955, McVicker's nephew, Joe McVicker, joined the company and began experimenting with the formula for the modeling compound. He made it more pliable and added a fresh, clean scent to it. He also changed the name of the product to "Play-Doh." Joe McVicker believed that the name would appeal to children and be easy for them to remember.

The new and improved Play-Doh was an immediate success. It was first sold in Cincinnati-area stores, where it quickly gained popularity. Within a few years, Play-Doh was being sold nationwide and was a staple of playtime for millions of children.

In the years that followed, Play-Doh continued to evolve and grow. The colors and scents of the product changed over time, and new accessories and tools were added to enhance the play experience. In the 1970s, Play-Doh became a cultural phenomenon, with commercials and advertising campaigns that cemented its place in popular culture.

Today, Play-Doh is owned by Hasbro and remains one of the most popular children's toys in the world. It is sold in over 80 countries and has inspired countless imitators and copycats. Play-Doh continues to be a staple of playtime for generations of children, inspiring creativity and imagination in young minds around the world.

One of the reasons for Play-Doh's enduring popularity is its versatility. Unlike many other toys that are designed for specific purposes or age groups, Play-Doh can be enjoyed by children of all ages and can be used in countless ways. From simple molding and shaping to more complex sculpting and modeling, Play-Doh can be used to create virtually anything a child can imagine.

Another reason for Play-Doh's success is its durability. Unlike many other children's toys that are quickly forgotten or discarded, Play-Doh can be reused and reshaped countless times. It is also non-toxic and safe for children to play with, which has made it a popular choice for parents and educators alike.

Over the years, Play-Doh has also been used in a variety of educational settings. Teachers and educators have found that the substance can be used to teach a wide range of subjects, including math, science, and art. Play-Doh has also been used in occupational therapy.

10 PUNCH

Punch is a beverage that has been enjoyed for centuries, and its origins can be traced back to India, where it was known as "panch" or "panchana," which means "five" in Hindi. The drink was originally made with five ingredients: alcohol, sugar, lemon, water, and tea or spices.

During the 17th and 18th centuries, punch became popular in England, where it was a staple at social gatherings and was often served in elaborate punch bowls. Punch was especially popular among the wealthy, who would often add expensive ingredients like brandy or champagne to their punch.

One of the most famous proponents of punch was Charles Dickens, who included references to the drink in several of his novels, including "A Christmas Carol" and "David Copperfield." Dickens was a great lover of punch and would often serve it to his guests at parties.

In the 19th century, the popularity of punch began to decline as other alcoholic beverages, such as wine and beer, became more widely available. However, punch continued to be served at social events and was a popular drink in the United States during the colonial era.

During Prohibition in the United States, which lasted from 1920 to 1933, punch experienced a resurgence in popularity as people turned to homemade alcohol to get their fix. Punch was also popular during World War II, when it was served to soldiers to boost morale.

Today, punch is still enjoyed around the world, and there are many different variations of the drink. Some modern versions of punch are made with fruit juices or soda, while others stick to the traditional ingredients of alcohol, sugar, lemon, water, and tea or spices.

In addition to its history as a popular beverage, punch has also played an important role in the social and cultural history of many countries. In England, for example, punch was often served at political rallies and was a symbol of patriotism and national pride.

In the United States, punch was a popular drink at colonial-era taverns, where it was often served to travelers and visitors. It was also a popular drink at political gatherings and was often used to bring people together and build community.

Today, punch continues to be a popular drink at social events, and there are many different recipes and variations to choose from. Whether you prefer a traditional punch made with alcohol and spices or a modern version made with fruit juice and soda, there is sure to be a punch recipe that will suit your taste.

11 ROCKING CHAIRS

Rocking chairs are a beloved piece of furniture that has been around for centuries. They have a rich history that spans multiple continents and cultures. From their humble beginnings as simple chairs to their current status as a symbol of comfort and relaxation, rocking chairs have come a long way.

The origins of rocking chairs can be traced back to the early 18th century in England. The first rocking chairs were not designed for comfort or relaxation, but rather as a tool for nursing mothers. The curved base of the chair allowed mothers to rock their babies to sleep while remaining seated and comfortable.

It wasn't until the mid-18th century that rocking chairs began to gain popularity as pieces of furniture. Benjamin Franklin is credited with introducing the rocking chair to the United States in the early 1700s. Franklin was a fan of the chair's gentle rocking motion and believed that it could help improve one's overall health and well-being.

In the 19th century, rocking chairs became a common fixture in American homes. They were especially popular in the South, where they were often used on front porches to provide relief from the sweltering heat. Rocking chairs were also commonly found in nursing homes and hospitals, where they were used to help soothe patients.

As the popularity of rocking chairs grew, so did the variety of designs available. Early rocking chairs were made primarily of wood and featured simple, straight lines. But as the 19th century progressed, rocking chairs became more ornate and decorative. They were often made of higher-quality wood and featured intricate carvings and decorations.

One of the most famous styles of rocking chairs is the Windsor rocking chair. This style originated in England in the early 18th century and was brought to America by early settlers. Windsor rocking chairs are known for their distinctive spindle backs and turned legs. They were often made of maple or birch and were popular in both rural and urban settings.

Another popular style of rocking chair is the Boston rocker. This style first appeared in the late 18th century and is characterized by its curved back and arms. Boston rockers were typically made of hardwoods like maple, oak, or cherry and were often painted or stained to enhance their beauty.

In the 20th century, rocking chairs continued to evolve. With the advent of new materials like steel and plastic, designers were able to create new and innovative designs. Rocking chairs became more streamlined and modern, with clean lines and minimal decoration.

Perhaps the most famous modern rocking chair is the Eames rocker. Designed by Charles and Ray Eames in the 1950s, this chair features a molded fiberglass seat and a wire base. It has become an icon of modern design and is still popular today.

Rocking chairs have also played a role in popular culture throughout the years. In the 19th century, they were often featured in works of art and literature. Edgar Allan Poe's poem "The Raven" famously includes the line, "Take thy beak from out my heart, and take thy form from off my door...quoth the Raven, 'Nevermore!'" as the narrator rocks nervously in his rocking chair. In the 20th century, rocking chairs were frequently featured in movies and television shows as a symbol of relaxation and comfort.

Today, rocking chairs remain a popular piece of furniture in homes around the world. They are used for everything from reading and watching television to nursing babies and soothing the elderly. With their rich history and enduring popularity, rocking chairs are sure to remain a beloved fixture in homes for years to come.

12 VIAGRA

Viagra, the famous blue pill used to treat erectile dysfunction, has become a household name since its introduction in 1998. The drug's discovery and development can be traced back to a series of scientific breakthroughs and innovations in the field of medicine.

The story of Viagra began in the early 1990s when scientists at Pfizer, a pharmaceutical company in the United States, were conducting research on a chemical compound called Sildenafil citrate. The compound was initially developed to treat angina, a condition characterized by chest pain and discomfort caused by insufficient blood flow to the heart.

During the clinical trials of Sildenafil citrate, researchers noticed an unexpected side effect of the drug. Men who took the drug reported improved erections, leading the scientists to hypothesize that the compound could also be used to treat erectile dysfunction, a condition in which men have difficulty achieving or maintaining an erection during sexual activity.

The potential of Sildenafil citrate as a treatment for erectile dysfunction sparked great interest among Pfizer's researchers, who began to conduct further tests on the drug.

Pfizer conducted a series of clinical trials to test the effectiveness and safety of Sildenafil citrate as a treatment for erectile dysfunction. In 1996, the company submitted a New Drug Application (NDA) to the US Food and Drug Administration (FDA) for the drug, which was then named Viagra.

The FDA approved Viagra for use in the United States in 1998, making it the first oral medication for erectile dysfunction available to the public. The drug's launch was met with widespread media attention, with many news outlets reporting on the potential impact of Viagra on men's sexual health.

Viagra's introduction had a significant impact on society, particularly in the realm of sexual health. The drug's availability provided men with a safe and effective treatment for erectile dysfunction, a condition that had previously been stigmatized and often went untreated.

The success of Viagra also led to increased awareness and discussion of erectile dysfunction, helping to break down the stigma surrounding the condition. Many men who had previously been reluctant to seek treatment for their erectile dysfunction were now more willing to speak to their doctors about the issue and explore potential treatment options.

In addition to its impact on sexual health, Viagra also had significant economic implications. The drug became a massive commercial success for Pfizer, generating billions of dollars in revenue each year. It also spawned a new industry of competitors, with several other pharmaceutical companies developing their own erectile dysfunction medications to capture a share of the market.

Despite its widespread popularity, Viagra has also been the subject of criticism and controversy. Some have raised concerns about the drug's potential side effects, which can include headaches, dizziness, and nausea.

Others have criticized Viagra for perpetuating harmful societal norms around masculinity and sexuality. Critics argue that the drug reinforces the idea that male sexual performance is paramount and that men should be ashamed if they are unable to perform sexually.

While Viagra has faced criticism and controversy over the years, it remains a significant cultural phenomenon and a symbol of the ongoing evolution of society's attitudes toward sex and sexuality.

13 BAND-AIDS

Band-Aids are a part of modern first-aid kits, found in medicine cabinets and purses across the world. They are so common that it is easy to forget that they are a relatively recent invention. The history of Band-Aids provides insight into the evolution of medicine, the growth of consumer culture, and the importance of branding and marketing.

The story of Band-Aids begins in the early 20th century. In 1920, Earle Dickson, a cotton buyer for Johnson & Johnson, invented the first adhesive bandage. The idea came to him after noticing that his wife frequently cut her fingers while cooking. He realized that a small bandage with an adhesive strip would be more convenient than traditional bandages, which required a separate piece of tape to hold them in place.

Dickson's first prototype was made by attaching small pieces of gauze to strips of adhesive tape. He showed it to his boss, James Wood Johnson, who saw the potential in the product. The company began producing the bandages under the name "Band-Aids" in 1921.

Initially, Band-Aids were not a commercial success. They were seen as a luxury item and were marketed primarily to hospitals and doctors. However, Johnson & Johnson recognized the potential for a consumer market and began to focus on promoting the product to the general public.

One of the key marketing strategies was to advertise Band-Aids to protect against infection. At the time, infectious diseases were a major concern, and the idea of a product that could help prevent infection resonated with consumers. Johnson & Johnson also created colorful packaging and placed the bandages in small, convenient tins that could be easily carried in a purse or pocket.

The real breakthrough for Band-Aids came during World War II. The U.S. government purchased large quantities of the bandages for use by soldiers, and Johnson & Johnson produced millions of Band-Aids for the war effort. After the war, soldiers brought the bandages home with them, and they became a household item.

In the decades that followed, Band-Aids continued to evolve. The company introduced new shapes and sizes, including strips, circles, and squares. They also began to use new materials, such as plastic, to make the bandages more durable and flexible. In the 1950s, Johnson & Johnson began to produce Band-Aids with cartoon characters and other designs, making them even more appealing to children.

Another important development in the history of Band-Aids was the introduction of "sheer" bandages in the 1960s. These bandages were made with a transparent material that was nearly invisible on the skin. They were particularly popular among women who wanted to conceal cuts and scrapes without drawing attention to them.

Today, Band-Aids are available in a wide variety of styles and designs. There are Band-Aids for children, with characters from popular movies and TV shows, and there are Band-Aids for adults, with more subdued colors and patterns. Johnson & Johnson continues to innovate, introducing new materials and technologies to make Band-Aids more effective and comfortable.

The history of Band-Aids is a testament to the power of marketing and branding. Johnson & Johnson recognized the potential of the product and worked hard to create a consumer market. They used advertising, packaging, and design to make Band-Aids appealing to the general public, and they were successful in creating a household name.

Band-Aids are also a reminder of the importance of innovation. Earle Dickson's invention was a simple but brilliant solution to a common problem, and it has had a profound impact on public health. Johnson & Johnson's continued investment in research and development has helped to make Band-Aids even more effective and useful.

14 FORTUNE COOKIES

Fortune cookies are a dessert that has become synonymous with Chinese cuisine. They are often served at the end of meals in Chinese restaurants and are enjoyed by people of all ages. However, the history of fortune cookies is shrouded in mystery, and the origins of this delicious treat are not entirely clear.

One popular myth is that fortune cookies were invented in China centuries ago. According to this story, the Chinese would bake moon cakes with messages of encouragement hidden inside to lift the spirits of soldiers fighting against the Mongols. However, there is no evidence to support this claim, and it is more likely that fortune cookies originated in the United States.

The first recorded instance of fortune cookies being served in the United States was at the Japanese Tea Garden in San Francisco in the early 1900s. However, the origins of the fortune cookie are still disputed, and several different stories exist as to how they became a staple in Chinese American cuisine.

One theory is that fortune cookies were invented by a Japanese immigrant named Makoto Hagiwara, who was responsible for designing and maintaining the Japanese Tea Garden in San Francisco. Hagiwara was a skilled baker, and it is believed that he may have created fortune cookies to serve at the tea garden in the early 1900s.

Another theory is that fortune cookies were invented by David Jung, a Chinese immigrant who founded the Hong Kong Noodle Company in Los Angeles in 1916. Jung was a deeply spiritual man, and he believed that his fortune cookies could help spread positive messages and bring good luck to people who ate them. He began selling fortune cookies to Chinese restaurants throughout Los Angeles, and they quickly became popular among Chinese Americans.

Regardless of who invented fortune cookies, they quickly became a hit in Chinese American cuisine. By the 1920s, fortune cookies were being served in Chinese restaurants throughout the United States, and they had become an iconic part of the Chinese American dining experience.

During World War II, fortune cookies gained even more popularity as they were included in care packages sent to American soldiers overseas. The messages inside the cookies were meant to lift the spirits of the soldiers and provide them with a bit of comfort from home.

However, the popularity of fortune cookies has not been without controversy. Some Chinese Americans have criticized fortune cookies for perpetuating stereotypes about Chinese culture and for being a non-authentic Chinese food. In the 1960s, Chinese American activists began protesting the use of fortune cookies in Chinese restaurants, arguing that they were a symbol of cultural appropriation.

Despite these criticisms, fortune cookies remain a beloved dessert in Chinese American cuisine. Today, fortune cookies are mass-produced and sold in grocery stores and Chinese restaurants around the world. The messages inside the cookies have become a popular form of entertainment, with people often reading them out loud and sharing them with friends and family.

In recent years, there has been a growing trend of personalized fortune cookies, where customers can order custom messages to be printed inside the cookies. This has made fortune cookies even more popular as gifts for special occasions such as weddings, birthdays, and corporate events.

15 THE MICROWAVE

The microwave oven has become an essential appliance in modern kitchens, and it's hard to imagine a time when people couldn't cook, reheat or defrost food using this convenient tool. However, the history of the microwave oven is relatively recent, dating back to the early 20th century.

The first steps towards the creation of the microwave oven were made in the 1940s, during World War II. The U.S. military had been experimenting with radar systems, which used high-frequency radio waves to detect the presence of enemy aircraft. A man named Percy Spencer, who was working for the company Raytheon, noticed that a chocolate bar he had in his pocket had melted after he had been near a radar tube. Spencer hypothesized that the microwaves produced by the radar system were responsible for melting the chocolate. Intrigued by this idea, he began experimenting with food to see what other effects microwaves might have.

Spencer's experiments led to the development of the first microwave oven, which was called the Radarange. The first Radarange was huge and expensive, standing over six feet tall and weighing over 700 pounds. It was used primarily in commercial kitchens and other large food service establishments.

The Radarange was not an instant success, primarily because it was too large and expensive for home use. It wasn't until the mid-1960s that smaller, more affordable microwave ovens began to appear on the market. The first of these was the Amana Radarange, which was introduced in 1967. The Amana was smaller and more affordable than the original Radarange, and it quickly became popular with home cooks.

The 1970s saw the widespread adoption of the microwave oven, as more manufacturers began producing smaller, more affordable models. By the end of the decade, nearly every American home had a microwave oven.

Microwave ovens have come a long way since their inception. Early models were relatively simple and had limited features. Today's models are much more advanced, with a wide range of features and functions. Some of the features available on modern microwave ovens include convection cooking, grilling, and even air frying.

The development of the microwave oven has had a significant impact on the way we cook and eat. It has made it much easier to prepare meals quickly and efficiently, which has saved time for busy families. It has also allowed us to reheat leftovers and defrost frozen foods quickly and easily.

However, the use of microwave ovens has also been the subject of some controversy. Some people have expressed concerns that microwaving food can reduce its nutritional value, or even cause harmful substances to be produced. While there is some evidence to support these concerns, most experts agree that microwave ovens are safe to use and that they do not significantly impact the nutritional value of food.

Despite the controversy surrounding microwave ovens, they have become an essential tool in modern kitchens. They have saved countless hours of cooking time, and they have made it easier for people to prepare healthy and delicious meals at home. As technology continues to advance, it will be interesting to see what new features and capabilities are added to microwave ovens in the years to come.

16 POTATO CHIPS

Potato chips are a snack food enjoyed by millions around the world. They have a long and storied history that stretches back centuries, and the story of their invention is a fascinating one.

The story of potato chips begins in the early 19th century, in the United States. At the time, potatoes were a popular food item, but they were typically boiled or mashed. One day, a chef by the name of George Crum was working at a resort in Saratoga Springs, New York, when he received a complaint from a customer about his French fries. The customer claimed that they were too thick and soggy, and demanded a new batch.

Rather than simply making a new batch of fries, Crum decided to teach the customer a lesson. He sliced the potatoes as thin as possible, fried them until they were crispy, and then salted them heavily. To his surprise, the customer loved them, and soon the other guests at the resort were asking for "potato chips," as they became known.

From there, potato chips began to gain popularity across the United States, and by the early 20th century, they had become a staple snack food. Companies like Frito-Lay and Wise began producing their own versions of potato chips, and the snack became even more widely available.

During World War II, potato chips became a symbol of American patriotism. The government encouraged people to eat potato chips to support the war effort, and companies like Frito-Lay even printed special messages on their chip bags encouraging people to buy war bonds.

In the post-war era, potato chips continued to grow in popularity. New flavors were introduced, such as barbecue and sour cream and onion, and the snack became a staple at parties and social gatherings.

Today, potato chips are enjoyed all over the world, and they come in an astonishing variety of flavors and varieties. Some people prefer traditional salted chips, while others opt for more exotic flavors like dill pickle or jalapeño.

Despite their popularity, however, potato chips have faced criticism from some quarters. Many nutritionists argue that they are a highly processed food that is high in fat and salt and can contribute to obesity and other health problems.

In response to these criticisms, some companies have started to produce "healthier" versions of potato chips, made with ingredients like sweet potatoes or beets. These chips are often baked instead of fried and contain less fat and salt than traditional chips.

Despite these concerns, however, potato chips remain a beloved snack food, and their popularity shows no signs of waning. From their humble origins as a prank played by a disgruntled chef, potato chips have become an iconic food item that is enjoyed by millions around the world.

17 ESCALATORS

Escalators are a form of vertical transportation that has become a feature of modern architecture. These moving staircases make it possible to ascend and descend multiple floors in buildings without the need for stairs, elevators or lifts. The history of escalators can be traced back to the mid-19th century, and they have undergone numerous advancements and changes since then.

The first documented concept of an escalator was presented by a patent in 1859 by Nathan Ames, an American inventor. The patent was for "revolving stairs" which consisted of a series of flat steps attached to a continuous loop, like a conveyor belt. The idea was to provide a new and efficient way to move people between floors, particularly in factories and warehouses. Ames' design, however, was never built.

The next major development in the history of escalators came in 1892, when Jesse W. Reno, an American inventor and entrepreneur, designed and built the world's first working escalator. Reno's escalator was called the "Endless Conveyor" and consisted of a series of flat steps attached to a continuous loop of belts. The belt loop was powered by a motor, and the steps were pulled along with it, allowing people to stand on the moving stairs and be carried up or down.

The first installation of Reno's escalator was at the Old Iron Pier in Coney Island, New York. It was an instant success and quickly became a popular attraction, carrying more than 75,000 passengers in its first two weeks of operation. Following this success, Reno installed escalators in other locations across the United States, including amusement parks, department stores, and subway stations.

Despite the success of Reno's escalator, it was not without its problems. One issue was that the steps were made of wood, which could become slippery when wet, posing a safety risk to users. To address this issue, Charles Seeberger, a German engineer, developed a new type of escalator in 1897 that used metal steps instead of wood.

Seeberger's design was a significant improvement over Reno's escalator, and it quickly gained popularity across Europe. In 1900, the Paris Metro became the first subway system in the world to install Seeberger's escalator, which quickly became a symbol of modernity and technological progress.

In the early 20th century, escalators continued to be developed and improved. In 1906, Otis Elevator Company, one of the world's largest manufacturers of elevators and escalators, introduced a new type of escalator that used a truss system to support the steps, making it stronger and more durable. This design became the standard for escalators and remains in use today.

Another significant development in the history of escalators came in the 1920s, when they began to be installed in large department stores and office buildings. This led to a significant increase in demand for escalators, and many companies began to specialize in their manufacture and installation.

One such company was the Montgomery Elevator Company, which was founded in 1892 and began manufacturing escalators in 1920. Montgomery's escalators were known for their innovative designs, including the "up-down" escalator, which allowed people to travel in two directions on the same escalator.

In the mid-20th century, escalators continued to be developed and refined. One notable advancement was the introduction of safety features such as emergency stop buttons and safety skirts, which prevented people from getting caught in the moving parts of the escalator.

Today, escalators are an integral part of modern architecture and are found in a wide range of settings, from shopping malls and airports to subway stations and office buildings. Technology has continued to evolve, with modern escalators featuring advanced safety features and energy-efficient designs.

18 POST-IT-NOTES

Post-it notes are often found in modern offices, homes, and schools, but few people know their origin story. The invention of Post-it notes is a tale of innovation that spans several decades and involves a team of researchers at 3M, a Minnesota-based manufacturing company.

The story of Post-it notes began in the 1960s when Dr. Spencer Silver, a scientist at 3M, was working on developing a strong adhesive for aerospace applications. Dr. Silver was trying to create an adhesive that would stick to almost anything but could also be easily removed without leaving any residue. However, despite years of research, Dr. Silver was unable to develop the adhesive he was looking for.

In 1974, Dr. Silver gave a presentation on his work to his colleagues at 3M, but the presentation did not generate much interest. However, one of the attendees, a scientist named Art Fry, saw the potential of Dr. Silver's adhesive in a completely different context. Art Fry was a choir singer and was frustrated that his bookmarks kept falling out of his hymnal. He realized that Dr. Silver's adhesive could be used to create a bookmark that would stick to the page but could also be easily removed without damaging the paper.

Fry experimented with the adhesive, applying it to small pieces of paper, and found that it worked perfectly as a bookmark. However, the small pieces of paper were not very practical, and Fry wanted to develop a larger, more useful product. He experimented with different types of paper and found that the ideal paper for the adhesive was a type of paper that had been developed by 3M for use in its masking tape. This paper had a low-tack adhesive that allowed it to stick to surfaces without damaging them.

In 1977, 3M introduced the first Post-it notes, which were initially called "Press 'n Peel" bookmarks. The first Post-it notes were yellow and measured 3x3 inches. The notes were initially marketed to office workers to label documents and files without damaging them. However, the initial marketing campaign was not very successful, and 3M almost discontinued the product.

However, the popularity of Post-it notes began to grow in the 1980s, thanks in part to a successful marketing campaign that targeted college students. 3M began to introduce Post-it notes in different colors and sizes, which made them more appealing to a wider range of users. The company also introduced a dispenser that made it easier to use post-it notes, which further increased their popularity.

Over the years, Post-it notes have become a cultural icon and have been featured in movies, television shows, and even art exhibits. Post-it notes have been used for a variety of purposes, from reminders and to-do lists to artwork and even wedding proposals. Post-it notes have also become a symbol of creativity and innovation, and many people use them as a tool for brainstorming and idea generation.

Today, Post-it notes are available in a wide range of colors, sizes, and shapes, and they are used by millions of people around the world. Post-it notes have also inspired a wide range of products, from Post-it note holders and dispensers to apps that allow users to create virtual Post-it notes on their computer screens.

19 THE SANDWICH

The sandwich is a food item that is enjoyed by people all over the world. It is a simple meal that can be eaten on the go or enjoyed as part of a leisurely lunch. The history of the sandwich is a fascinating one that is steeped in tradition and innovation.

The origins of the sandwich can be traced back to the 18th century when John Montagu, the fourth Earl of Sandwich, popularized the idea of putting meat between two slices of bread. The story goes that the Earl was a passionate gambler who did not want to interrupt his game to eat a proper meal. So, he instructed his cook to prepare him a meal that he could eat while continuing to play cards. The cook took slices of beef and placed them between two slices of bread, creating what would become known as the "sandwich."

While the Earl of Sandwich is often credited with inventing the sandwich, the concept of putting food between bread had been around for centuries. In fact, the ancient Greeks and Romans had a similar dish that they called "trenchers." Trenchers were pieces of stale bread that were used as plates for meat and other foods. The bread would soak up the juices from the food, making it more flavorful and easier to eat.

The sandwich gained popularity in England and quickly spread to other parts of Europe and the United States. In the 19th century, the sandwich became a popular lunchtime meal in the United States, especially among factory workers and other laborers who needed a quick and convenient meal. Sandwich shops began to pop up in cities all over the country, offering a variety of sandwich options to hungry customers.

One of the most famous sandwiches in American history is the peanut butter and jelly sandwich. The combination of peanut butter and jelly on bread became popular in the early 20th century and remains a staple in many American households to this day. The sandwich was especially popular during World War II when meat was rationed, and families needed a cheap and nutritious meal.

In the 1960s and 1970s, the sandwich underwent a transformation as more exotic ingredients were introduced. Sandwiches filled with avocado, hummus, and other non-traditional ingredients became popular, especially among health-conscious consumers. The sandwich also became a popular item on restaurant menus, with chefs experimenting with different breads, fillings, and sauces to create unique and flavorful sandwich options.

Today, the sandwich continues to be a popular meal all over the world. From the classic peanut butter and jelly sandwich to more elaborate creations like the Reuben or the club sandwich, there is a sandwich to suit every taste and occasion. Sandwich shops and delis continue to thrive, offering customers a wide variety of sandwich options made with fresh ingredients and creative flavor combinations.

In recent years, there has been a growing trend toward healthier, more sustainable sandwich options. Restaurants and sandwich shops are using locally sourced and organic ingredients to create sandwiches that are not only delicious but also environmentally friendly. There has also been a surge in plant-based sandwich options, with restaurants and sandwich shops offering vegetarian and vegan options to cater to customers who are looking for healthier and more sustainable meal options.

20 POCKETS

Pockets are an essential feature of clothing that we often take for granted. They are incredibly useful for carrying items such as keys, phones, wallets, and more. However, the history of pockets is more complex than you might think.

The earliest evidence of pockets dates to ancient times. The ancient Greeks and Romans used small pouches called "subligacula" to carry personal items. These pouches were attached to a belt and worn around the waist. However, these pouches were not attached to clothing, and as such, they were not true pockets.

It was not until the Middle Ages that pockets started to resemble the ones we know today. During this time, men and women wore fitted garments with slits in the side seams that provided access to a small pocket sewn into the lining. These pockets were used to carry personal items such as money, keys, and small tools.

During the Renaissance period, men's clothing became more elaborate, and pockets became larger and more decorative. The ornate pockets on men's clothing were a symbol of wealth and status. Women's clothing, on the other hand, remained relatively simple, with small pockets sewn into the seams of their skirts.

In the 17th century, clothing styles became even more elaborate, and pockets became even more important. Men's clothing featured large pockets that were often decorated with embroidery or other embellishments. These pockets were often so large that they could be used to carry a variety of items, including books and even food.

However, women's clothing did not keep up with the trend for larger pockets. Instead, women's pockets became smaller and were often hidden under layers of petticoats and skirts. This was partly because women's clothing became more form-fitting during this time, and large pockets would have ruined the silhouette.

During the 18th century, pockets underwent a significant change. Men's clothing became simpler, and pockets became smaller and more practical. The large ornate pockets of the previous century were replaced with smaller pockets that were sewn directly into the garment. This made the pockets more secure and less likely to snag on objects.

Women's clothing also underwent a change during this time. The pocket was removed from the skirt entirely and replaced with a small bag called a reticule. The reticule was carried in the hand and was used to carry personal items such as fans, handkerchiefs, and makeup.

The 19th century saw further changes to pocket design. Men's clothing continued to feature small pockets, but they became more numerous. The pocket watch became popular during this time, and men's clothing often featured a small pocket specifically designed to hold a watch.

Women's clothing also saw changes during this time. The reticule was replaced with a small pocket sewn into the waistband of the skirt. This allowed women to carry personal items without having to hold a bag in their hand.

During the 20th century, pockets became more standardized. Men's clothing continued to feature small pockets, but they were often placed in the front of the garment. This made them more accessible and allowed for easier access to personal items.

Women's clothing also saw changes during this time. Skirts became shorter, and pants became more popular for women. Pants featured pockets that were like men's pants, and women's clothing finally had pockets that were functional and practical.

In the 21st century, pockets have become an integral part of clothing design. Both men's and women's clothing feature pockets that are practical and functional. Clothing designers have found new and innovative ways to incorporate pockets into their designs, and pockets have become an important selling point for many clothing brands.

21 BLUE JEANS

The history of blue jeans can be traced back to the mid-19th century when denim fabric was first used to make durable work clothes for miners, cowboys, and laborers. However, it was not until the early 20th century that blue jeans became a popular fashion item, worn by people from all walks of life.

The story of blue jeans began in the 1850s when a German immigrant named Levi Strauss arrived in San Francisco, California. Strauss was a businessman who sold dry goods and clothing, and he recognized the need for durable work clothes for the miners who were working in the gold mines of California. Strauss teamed up with a tailor named Jacob Davis, and together they designed a pair of pants made from a sturdy fabric called denim.

The first pair of blue jeans was created in 1873 when Strauss and Davis received a patent for the design of riveted work pants. The rivets were placed at points of stress to reinforce the fabric and make the pants more durable. The original blue jeans had one back pocket, a watch pocket, and a button fly. They were made from a heavy-weight denim fabric that was dyed blue with indigo.

At first, blue jeans were primarily worn by laborers and cowboys. They were practical, durable, and affordable, making them ideal for people who worked hard and needed clothes that could withstand wear and tear. However, blue jeans began to gain popularity beyond the working class in the 1930s and 1940s. Hollywood movies often depicted cowboys and other rugged characters wearing blue jeans, which helped to make them more fashionable.

During World War II, blue jeans became a symbol of American culture as soldiers stationed overseas often wore them as part of their uniform. When the war ended, many soldiers returned home with a new appreciation for blue jeans, and the trend continued to grow. By the 1950s, blue jeans had become a fashion statement, particularly among teenagers.

In the 1960s and 1970s, blue jeans became a symbol of rebellion and counterculture. The hippie movement embraced blue jeans as a symbol of anti-establishment and individuality. The style evolved as bell-bottom jeans became popular, with flared legs and embroidered designs.

In the 1980s, blue jeans became mainstream once again, with designer brands like Calvin Klein and Gloria Vanderbilt creating high-end versions of the classic pants. The rise of hip hop culture also brought a new style of blue jeans, with baggy, oversized jeans becoming popular among urban youth.

Today, blue jeans are a staple of fashion around the world. They come in a variety of styles, from classic straight-leg jeans to skinny jeans and boyfriend jeans. They can be dressed up or dressed down, worn with heels or sneakers, and are suitable for nearly any occasion.

One reason for the enduring popularity of blue jeans is their versatility. They are comfortable enough for everyday wear yet can be dressed up for a night out. They are also available in a range of price points, from affordable options to high-end designer jeans.

Another reason for the popularity of blue jeans is their association with American culture. Jeans are often seen as a symbol of freedom, individuality, and self-expression. They are also associated with the American West, and the rugged, independent spirit that has long been associated with that region.

In recent years, the fashion industry has become increasingly concerned with sustainability and ethical practices. Many companies have begun to focus on producing eco-friendly jeans, using organic cotton and other sustainable materials. Some companies have also started to focus on fair labor practices, ensuring that the workers who produce their jeans are paid fair wages and work in safe conditions.

Despite their long history, blue jeans continue to be a fashion staple for people around the world.

22 FROZEN FOODS

The history of frozen food can be traced back to the early 20th century when Clarence Birdseye, an American inventor, developed a process to freeze fish while he was working in Labrador, Canada. Birdseye observed that the Inuit people used to freeze fish quickly in sub-zero temperatures to preserve them. Inspired by this, he developed a process to freeze food quickly, locking in its freshness and flavor.

In 1923, Birdseye established the General Seafood Corporation in Gloucester, Massachusetts, and started selling his frozen fish products. However, frozen food did not gain widespread acceptance until the 1940s, when World War II broke out.

During the war, the demand for food increased, and the government needed a way to preserve food for soldiers overseas. Frozen food became a practical solution as it could be transported easily and stored for long periods. In 1945, the United States Department of Agriculture launched the "Frozen Food for Freedom" campaign, encouraging people to eat frozen food to help the war effort.

After the war, frozen food became popular among consumers as well. The convenience and time-saving benefits of frozen food appealed to busy homemakers who wanted to spend less time preparing meals. Manufacturers began developing a wide range of frozen food products, including vegetables, fruits, meats, and prepared meals.

One of the most significant advancements in the frozen food industry was the introduction of the TV dinner in 1954 by Swanson. The TV dinner was a pre-packaged, frozen meal that could be heated in the oven and served on a tray. It was designed to be eaten in front of the television, hence the name. The TV dinner became an instant hit, and by 1960, Swanson was selling more than ten million TV dinners a year.

In the 1960s and 1970s, the frozen food industry continued to grow, and new technologies were developed to improve the quality and variety of frozen food products. The introduction of blast freezing allowed for faster freezing, resulting in better quality frozen food. Microwave ovens also became popular during this time, making it easier for consumers to heat and serve frozen food quickly.

In the 1980s, concerns about health and nutrition led to a shift in consumer demand for healthier frozen food options. Manufacturers began developing low-fat and low-calorie frozen meals, and the industry saw a rise in sales of frozen vegetables and fruits.

Today, the frozen food industry is a multibillion-dollar industry, with a wide range of products available for consumers. Frozen food has become an essential part of modern life, providing a convenient and cost-effective way to prepare meals at home. The industry continues to evolve, with new technologies and innovations being developed to improve the quality and variety of frozen food products.

23 CHOCOLATE CHIP COOKIES

The chocolate chip cookie is a classic American dessert that has become a staple in households all over the world. The origin of this delicious treat can be traced back to the 1930s, and the creation of the Toll House Inn, a popular restaurant in Whitman, Massachusetts.

The Toll House Inn was owned by Ruth Wakefield, a skilled baker and chef, who was known for her homemade desserts. In 1930, while preparing a batch of Butter Drop Do cookies, Ruth realized she was out of baker's chocolate, which she typically used in her recipe. In a stroke of genius, she substituted broken pieces of Nestle semi-sweet chocolate bars into her cookie dough, hoping the chocolate would melt and spread evenly throughout the cookie. To her surprise, the chocolate retained its shape, resulting in a delicious combination of crisp cookie and soft chocolate.

The chocolate chip cookie was an instant hit, and customers couldn't get enough of Ruth's creation. As word of the cookie spread, Nestle approached Ruth with a proposition - they would provide her with all the chocolate she needed for her cookies, and in exchange, they could feature her recipe on their chocolate bar packaging. Ruth agreed, and the recipe for Toll House Cookies appeared on Nestle chocolate packaging for years to come.

The popularity of the chocolate chip cookie only continued to grow, and it wasn't long before other bakers began incorporating this delicious ingredient into their own recipes. In fact, by the 1940s, chocolate chip cookies had become a staple dessert in many American households.

Over the years, variations of the classic chocolate chip cookie have emerged, including double chocolate chip cookies, oatmeal chocolate chip cookies, and even gluten-free and vegan versions. Despite these changes, the original recipe for Toll House Cookies remains a favorite among many bakers and cookie lovers.

Today, chocolate chip cookies can be found in bakeries, grocery stores, and households all over the world. While the chocolate chip cookie may have started as a simple substitution in a recipe, it has since become a beloved dessert that has stood the test of time.

In addition to its delicious taste, the chocolate chip cookie has also had an impact on the world of food and business. Ruth Wakefield's creation sparked a partnership with Nestle that continues to this day, and her recipe has become a cultural icon in American cuisine. Furthermore, the popularity of the chocolate chip cookie has led to the creation of countless baking and cooking shows, as well as a variety of cookbooks that focus solely on this beloved dessert.

The history of the chocolate chip cookie is a testament to the power of innovation and creativity in the culinary world. What started as a simple substitution in a cookie recipe has become a cultural icon that has influenced the way we think about and consume desserts. Whether enjoyed with a glass of milk, a cup of coffee, or on its own, the chocolate chip cookie will always hold a special place in the hearts and taste buds of people all over the world.

24 THE SLINKY

The Slinky is a classic toy that has been enjoyed by generations of children and adults alike. The toy is essentially a helical spring that is made of metal or plastic, and it can be stretched and compressed to perform a variety of tricks and movements. The Slinky is a versatile toy that has captivated the imaginations of people around the world since it was first invented in the 1940s.

The Slinky was invented by Richard James, an engineer who was working on a project to develop springs that could be used to stabilize sensitive instruments on ships during rough seas. One day in 1943, he accidentally knocked one of the springs off his workbench and watched as it "walked" down a series of books and onto the floor. He was intrigued by the way the spring moved and realized that it could be turned into a toy.

Richard James spent the next several years developing the Slinky, experimenting with different materials and sizes until he finally settled on a design that was both durable and flexible. The first Slinky was made from 80 feet of wire that was cut into a 2.5-inch-long coil. The toy was an instant success when it was introduced at a Gimbels department store in Philadelphia in 1945. The Slinky sold out within 90 minutes, and James knew that he had a hit on his hands.

The Slinky quickly became a cultural phenomenon in the United States, and it was soon being sold in toy stores across the country. Children loved the toy because it was easy to use and could perform a wide variety of tricks, while adults appreciated its simple yet elegant design. The Slinky was even featured in several popular movies and television shows, including "Toy

Story," "The Simpsons," and "The Wonder Years."

Over the years, the Slinky has undergone a few changes and improvements. In the 1960s, James introduced a plastic version of the toy that was lighter and cheaper to produce than the original metal version. This allowed the Slinky to be sold in even more stores and to reach an even wider audience. In the 1990s, a giant Slinky was introduced that was more than two feet in diameter and could be used as a decoration or as a toy.

Despite its popularity, the Slinky has faced its fair share of challenges over the years. In the late 1960s, Richard James left his wife and six children to join a religious cult, leaving his business partner to run the company. The company struggled for several years before being bought by a new owner who was able to revive its fortunes.

In the 21st century, the Slinky has faced competition from a wide variety of new toys and gadgets. However, the Slinky remains a beloved classic that is still enjoyed by people of all ages. In fact, the toy has even been used in scientific experiments to study the physics of springs and how they move.

Today, the Slinky is still being produced by the original manufacturer, James Industries, and is sold in stores around the world. The company has expanded its line of toys to include a variety of different sizes and colors of Slinkies, as well as other toys and games. The Slinky has become more than just a toy; it is now an iconic symbol of American culture that has been enjoyed by generations of people.

25 LIPSTICK

Lipstick has a long history, dating back to ancient times. Throughout the ages, lipstick has been used as a symbol of beauty, wealth, and power.

The earliest known use of lipstick dates to ancient Mesopotamia, around 5000 BC. At that time, women used crushed gemstones to decorate their lips. The gemstones were ground into a fine powder and mixed with oils or animal fats to create a paste that could be applied to the lips. This practice was also common in ancient Egypt, where women used a red pigment made from crushed carmine beetles mixed with beeswax to color their lips.

Lipstick also played a significant role in ancient Greece and Rome. In Greece, women applied red pigment to their lips and cheeks, while in Rome, women used a combination of red ochre and vermillion to color their lips. It was believed that lipstick had both aesthetic and medicinal properties, and it was commonly used to protect the lips from the harsh Mediterranean climate.

During the Middle Ages, lipstick fell out of fashion in Europe, and it was not until the Renaissance that the trend began to re-emerge. In the 16th century, Queen Elizabeth I of England was known for her signature red lips. She would apply a mixture of beeswax and red pigment to her lips, and she even banned her ladies-in-waiting from wearing red lipstick, reserving the color for herself.

The popularity of lipstick continued to grow throughout the 18th and 19th centuries. During the French Revolution, red lipstick became a symbol of rebellion, and women would wear it as a sign of their allegiance to the revolution. In the 19th century, lipstick became more widely available, as it was mass-produced and sold in small containers.

The early 20th century saw a significant shift in the way lipstick was marketed and sold. In 1912, the first modern lipstick was invented by Maurice Levy, and it was sold in a metal tube. This made it more convenient for women to apply lipstick on the go, and it also made it more hygienic, as the tube could be easily cleaned.

During the 1920s, the "flapper" style became popular, and women began to wear bolder, more dramatic makeup. Lipstick was a key part of this look, and women would wear dark, matte colors, often with a cupid's bow shape on their upper lip. In the 1930s, Hollywood glamour influenced the style of lipstick, with actresses like Marilyn Monroe and Elizabeth Taylor sporting bold red lips.

During World War II, lipstick became a symbol of patriotism, as women were encouraged to wear bright red lipstick to boost morale. However, during the post-war years, lipstick fell out of fashion, as women focused on more natural, understated looks.

In the 1960s and 1970s, the popularity of lipstick began to grow again, with women experimenting with bold colors and textures. In the 1980s, bright, neon-colored lipstick was popular, and women would often wear multiple colors at once, creating a rainbow effect on their lips.

In recent years, lipstick has become more diverse than ever before. There are now thousands of shades and textures available, from matte to glossy, and from natural to bold. The rise of social media has also had a significant impact on the way lipstick is marketed and sold, with influencers and celebrities promoting their favorite brands and colors to their millions of followers.

26 COTTON SWABS

Cotton swabs, also known as cotton buds or Q-tips, have been a staple in households and medical settings for decades. These small sticks with cotton balls on each end have a long and interesting history that dates back centuries.

The ancient Egyptians are credited with inventing the first cotton swabs, which were used for cleaning the ears. They would use a hollow reed filled with oil to clean out their ears, and then use a small piece of linen or cotton to remove the excess oil. However, it wasn't until the 1920s that the modern cotton swab was created.

In 1923, a Polish-American inventor named Leo Gerstenzang noticed his wife using cotton balls to clean their baby's ears. He saw that the cotton balls were too large and often fell apart, leaving pieces of cotton in the baby's ear. Gerstenzang decided to create a better tool for cleaning ears and came up with the idea of a cotton swab. He named his invention "Q-tip," which stands for "quality tip."

Gerstenzang's Q-tips were made by wrapping cotton around a wooden stick, like the way modern cotton swabs are made. He began selling Q-tips in 1926 and they quickly became popular with parents and healthcare professionals. By the 1930s, Q-tips were being used for a variety of purposes, including cleaning wounds and applying medication.

During World War II, cotton swabs became an essential tool for soldiers in the field. They were used to clean weapons and equipment, as well as to treat minor injuries. After the war, cotton swabs became more widely available and were used by consumers for a variety of purposes.

In the 1950s, the use of cotton swabs in the medical field expanded. They were used to collect samples for laboratory testing and to apply medication directly to the affected area. Cotton swabs also became a popular tool for artists, who used them to create detailed drawings and paintings.

By the 1960s, Q-tips had become a household name and were being used for a wide range of applications. They were used to clean computer equipment, apply makeup, and even as a substitute for paintbrushes. However, concerns began to arise about the safety of using cotton swabs to clean ears.

In the 1970s, doctors began warning against the use of cotton swabs for ear cleaning. They pointed out that using cotton swabs to clean ears could push wax deeper into the ear canal, leading to impaction and potential hearing loss. Despite these warnings, many people continued to use cotton swabs for ear cleaning.

In the 1980s, Q-tips underwent a redesign to address safety concerns. The wooden stick was replaced with a plastic stick, which was less likely to break and leave a piece of wood in the ear canal. The cotton on the ends of the swabs was also made softer and more absorbent, making them more effective for cleaning and applying medication.

Today, cotton swabs are used for a wide range of applications. They are still used for ear cleaning, but are also used for applying makeup, cleaning computer equipment, and applying medication. Some cotton swabs are even coated with a solution to clean teeth and freshen breath.

In recent years, there has been a push to reduce the use of disposable cotton swabs in favor of reusable alternatives. This is because disposable cotton swabs can contribute to plastic waste and pollution. Reusable cotton swabs are made from materials like silicone or bamboo and can be washed and reused multiple times.

27 BOTTLED WATER

Bottled water has become an essential commodity for many people today, with a global market worth billions of dollars. It is hard to imagine a time when drinking water came from anything other than a tap or a well. However, the history of bottled water is a relatively recent phenomenon that dates to the early 17th century.

The first known instance of bottled water dates to 1622 when the British scientist Sir Francis Bacon discovered a natural spring in the town of Epsom in England. He noticed that the water had healing properties and decided to bottle it for medicinal purposes. Bacon's discovery marked the beginning of the bottled water industry, and it quickly gained popularity across Europe.

However, it wasn't until the late 18th century that bottled water became more widely available. In 1767, a Frenchman named Philippe Henri de Girard invented the first corked glass bottle, which made it possible to transport water over long distances without it spoiling. The corked glass bottle was a significant innovation that allowed water to be bottled and transported in large quantities.

The first bottled water company was established in the United States in 1809 by a man named Jackson. He began bottling the water from a mineral spring in New York, which he believed had medicinal properties. The company quickly gained popularity, and other companies soon followed suit.

In the 19th century, bottled water became a popular drink among the upper classes. People believed that water from natural springs and wells had healing properties and was a healthier alternative to the contaminated water found in cities. As a result, many companies sprang up around the world, bottling water from natural springs and wells.

However, the popularity of bottled water declined in the early 20th century with the widespread availability of treated tap water. Tap water was just as safe and healthy as bottled water, and it was much cheaper. As a result, many bottled water companies went out of business.

The bottled water industry experienced a resurgence in the 1970s with the introduction of plastic bottles. Plastic bottles were cheaper and lighter than glass bottles, making them easier to transport and more convenient for consumers. In addition, advances in technology allowed companies to purify and filter tap water, making it taste better than ever before.

The 1980s saw the emergence of the bottled water industry as we know it today. Companies like Perrier and Evian began marketing their products as luxury items, targeting the upper classes with high-quality packaging and branding. The marketing campaigns were successful, and bottled water quickly became a status symbol.

In the 1990s, bottled water sales exploded as the health and fitness craze swept the world. People began to view bottled water as a healthier alternative to sugary drinks and as an essential component of a healthy lifestyle. The industry responded by introducing flavored and vitamin-enriched water, as well as functional water that claimed to have additional health benefits.

Today, the bottled water industry is a multi-billion-dollar business, with hundreds of brands and varieties available worldwide. Despite its popularity, bottled water is not without controversy. Critics argue that it is wasteful, with millions of plastic bottles ending up in landfills every year. Others argue that bottled water is no safer or healthier than tap water and that it is simply a marketing gimmick.

In response to these criticisms, many bottled water companies have started to use more sustainable packaging, such as biodegradable bottles and recycled materials. Some companies have even begun to focus on local sourcing, bottling water from natural sources close to their production facilities to reduce transportation costs.

28 BALLPOINT PENS

The ballpoint pen, also known as a biro, is a writing instrument that has become universal in modern society. Its origins can be traced back to the late 19th century, when inventors began to experiment with different ways of creating a pen that would be easy to use and not prone to leaking. However, it was not until the mid-20th century that the ballpoint pen became a popular consumer item.

The first patent for a ballpoint pen was issued to John Loud in 1888. Loud's design involved a small rotating ball that would pick up ink from a reservoir and transfer it to paper as it rolled across the page. However, the pen was not a commercial success, as the ball was prone to jamming and the ink would often leak.

In the early 20th century, other inventors began to experiment with ballpoint pen designs. In 1938, László Bíró and his brother Georg, both Hungarian journalists, developed a pen with a tiny ball bearing in its tip that would rotate as the pen was moved across the paper. The ball would pick up ink from a reservoir and transfer it to the paper, creating a smooth, consistent line.

Bíró's design was an improvement over earlier ballpoint pens, as it was less prone to jamming and leaking. In 1940, the Bíró brothers patented their design and began to produce pens under the name "Bíró Pens." These pens were initially popular with the British Royal Air Force, as they could write at high altitudes without leaking or smudging.

However, the Bíró pen was not an immediate commercial success. The cost of the pen was high, and it was not until after World War II that the ballpoint pen began to gain widespread popularity. In the United States, the

Eversharp Company began to produce ballpoint pens in the early 1940s, and by the mid-1950s, they had become the dominant type of pen in the country.

One reason for the ballpoint pen's popularity was its versatility. Unlike fountain pens, which required careful handling and maintenance, ballpoint pens were rugged and easy to use. They could write on almost any surface and were not affected by changes in temperature or pressure.

Another factor in the ballpoint pen's success was its convenience. Unlike fountain pens, which required constant refilling, ballpoint pens could hold a large amount of ink and would last for months or even years without needing to be refilled. This made them ideal for use in offices and other settings where a large amount of writing was required.

Over the years, the ballpoint pen has undergone numerous improvements and refinements. The ink used in ballpoint pens has become more reliable and consistent, and the pens themselves have become lighter and more comfortable to hold. Today, ballpoint pens are available in a wide variety of colors and styles, and they remain one of the most popular writing instruments in the world.

29 BARCODES

Barcodes have become an indispensable part of our daily lives. They are often found in retail, healthcare, logistics, and many other sectors. However, the history of barcodes is not as straightforward as their current prevalence might suggest. The development of barcodes is a story of technological innovation, industrial competition, and standardization efforts that spanned several decades.

The earliest predecessors of modern barcodes can be traced back to the late 1940s and early 1950s. At that time, the grocery industry was booming, but retailers were struggling to keep up with the demand for faster and more accurate checkout processes. The prevailing method for tracking inventory was manual, with clerks counting items by hand and entering prices into registers. This process was slow and error-prone, leading to long lines and dissatisfied customers.

To address this issue, several inventors began experimenting with automated checkout systems. One of the earliest pioneers was Joseph Woodland, a graduate student at Drexel University. In 1948, Woodland was sitting on a Florida beach, drawing patterns in the sand, when he came up with the idea of using a series of lines of varying thickness to represent data. He patented his idea in 1952, but it would be several more decades before his invention gained widespread acceptance.

In the meantime, other inventors were also exploring the potential of automated checkout systems. In 1951, Norman Joseph Woodland and Bernard Silver, two graduate students at the University of Pennsylvania, filed a patent for a "Classifying Apparatus and Method." Their system used circular symbols printed on paper, which could be read by a photodetector and converted into electrical signals. Although this technology was promising, it was expensive to produce and difficult to read accurately.

It wasn't until the 1960s that barcodes began to take shape in their modern form. In 1966, a group of grocery industry executives approached the National Association of Food Chains (NAFC) with a proposal to develop a standard barcode system. They recognized that a standardized system would be essential for widespread adoption, as retailers would need to be able to scan barcodes from different manufacturers and suppliers.

The NAFC formed a committee to study the issue, and in 1970, they published a set of specifications for a universal product code (UPC). The UPC system used a series of black and white bars of varying widths to represent numerical data. The bars were read by a photodetector and converted into electrical signals, which could be interpreted by a computer. The UPC system was designed to be simple, reliable, and easy to implement, and it quickly gained widespread acceptance in the retail industry.

The first product to be sold with a UPC barcode was a pack of Wrigley's chewing gum, which was scanned at a supermarket in Ohio on June 26, 1974. From that point on, the use of barcodes exploded, as retailers realized the benefits of automated checkout systems. Barcodes allowed for faster and more accurate transactions, reduced the need for manual data entry, and provided valuable data on inventory levels and sales trends.

In the years that followed, the use of barcodes continued to expand into new industries and applications. In healthcare, barcodes were used to track patient records, medication dosages, and medical devices. In logistics, barcodes were used to track packages, shipments, and inventory levels. Barcodes were even used in amusement parks and museums, where they could be scanned to provide information on exhibits and attractions.

As the use of barcodes became more widespread, so did the need for standardization. In 1981, the International Organization for Standardization (ISO) published a set of guidelines for barcode symbology, which outlined the specifications for several different types of barcodes.

30 THE AIR CONDITIONER

The invention of air conditioning systems revolutionized the way we live, work, and play. It is difficult to imagine life without the comfort and convenience that air conditioning provides, but this technology is relatively new. The history of air conditioning dates to the 1800s, and its development and evolution have been driven by changing needs, innovations in technology, and a desire for greater comfort.

The first air conditioning system was not intended for human comfort, but rather to control humidity in a printing press. In 1902, Willis Carrier, a young engineer, developed the first modern air conditioning system while working for the Buffalo Forge Company in New York. Carrier's system was designed to regulate the temperature and humidity in a printing plant, but it quickly became clear that the technology had potential for other applications.

The first residential air conditioning unit was installed in 1914 in Minneapolis, Minnesota. The system was designed by Charles Gates, who worked for the company that later became known as Honeywell. The unit was massive, taking up an entire basement, but it was a significant step forward in the development of air conditioning.

Air conditioning technology was further developed during World War II when the US Army needed to cool equipment and spaces in tropical regions. The need for air conditioning in commercial buildings also increased during this time as offices and businesses became more prevalent. As a result, air conditioning became more affordable and accessible.

In the 1950s and 1960s, air conditioning became a common feature in homes and cars. As more people moved to warmer regions of the country, air conditioning became a necessity rather than a luxury. The development of new refrigerants also made air conditioning systems more efficient and affordable.

In the 1970s, concern over energy consumption and environmental impact led to the development of new air conditioning technologies. One such innovation was the introduction of the heat pump, which allowed for both heating and cooling in a single system. Heat pumps are much more energy-efficient than traditional heating and cooling systems, making them a popular choice for homeowners.

Today, air conditioning is everywhere in many parts of the world. Technology has advanced to the point where air conditioning systems can be controlled remotely, and even learn the habits and preferences of the people who use them. The widespread use of air conditioning has changed the way we live, work, and play, allowing us to be comfortable in even the hottest and most humid environments.

While air conditioning has brought many benefits, there are also drawbacks. The energy consumption required to run air conditioning systems has a significant impact on the environment, contributing to greenhouse gas emissions and climate change. There is also concern about the use of refrigerants, which can be harmful to the environment if they leak into the atmosphere.

As a result, efforts are being made to develop more energy-efficient air conditioning systems and to find alternatives to traditional refrigerants. In recent years, researchers have explored the use of natural refrigerants such as carbon dioxide, ammonia, and propane. These refrigerants are less harmful to the environment and can be more energy-efficient than traditional refrigerants.

31 ANTISEPTICS

Antiseptics are substances that are used to prevent the growth and reproduction of microorganisms on living tissue. They have been used throughout history to prevent infection and promote healing, but it wasn't until the mid-19th century that antiseptics became an integral part of medical practice.

The use of antiseptics dates to ancient times. Many ancient civilizations, such as the Egyptians, Greeks, and Romans, used various substances to clean wounds and prevent infection. For example, the Egyptians used honey and lard as topical treatments, while the Greeks used vinegar and wine as antiseptics.

During the Middle Ages, the use of antiseptics declined, and many medical practices became more reliant on superstition and tradition rather than science. However, the Renaissance brought a renewed interest in science and medicine, and the use of antiseptics began to re-emerge.

In the 18th century, a Scottish surgeon named John Hunter began to experiment with various substances to prevent infection. He found that applying vinegar to wounds helped prevent infection, and he also discovered that boric acid had antiseptic properties.

It wasn't until the mid-19th century that antiseptics became an integral part of medical practice, thanks to the work of Joseph Lister. Lister was a British surgeon who became interested in preventing infection after seeing the devastating effects of postoperative infections. He believed that infections were caused by microorganisms that entered the body during surgery and set out to find a way to prevent them.

Lister's experiments led him to discover that carbolic acid (now known as phenol) had strong antiseptic properties. He began to use carbolic acid to clean wounds and surgical instruments, and he also began to apply it to his hands and clothing before performing surgery. Lister's use of carbolic acid led to a significant decrease in postoperative infections, and his methods became known as antiseptic surgery.

Lister's work revolutionized the field of surgery and had a significant impact on medical practice. His methods were widely adopted, and the use of antiseptics became standard practice in hospitals around the world.

After the discovery of carbolic acid, researchers began to experiment with other substances to find new and more effective antiseptics. In 1867, a French chemist named Louis Pasteur discovered that heat could be used to kill microorganisms, which led to the development of sterilization techniques. Other researchers began to experiment with various chemicals, such as hydrogen peroxide, iodine, and chlorine, as antiseptics.

In 1892, an English bacteriologist named Alexander Fleming discovered the antiseptic properties of a substance called lysozyme. Lysozyme is an enzyme found in tears and other bodily fluids that can break down bacterial cell walls, making it an effective natural antiseptic.

In the early 20th century, researchers began to experiment with the use of chemicals to kill bacteria, leading to the discovery of antibiotics. In 1928, Alexander Fleming discovered that a mold called Penicillium notatum produced a substance that could kill bacteria. This substance became known as penicillin, and it was the first antibiotic to be discovered.

The discovery of antibiotics revolutionized medicine and had a significant impact on the use of antiseptics. Antibiotics are more effective than antiseptics at killing bacteria, and they have fewer side effects.

32 BATTERIES

The history of batteries dates to ancient times, when people used primitive forms of batteries for medical treatments and religious ceremonies. However, the modern battery, as we know it today, was invented in the 19th century and has since revolutionized the world by providing portable energy for everything from flashlights to electric cars.

The earliest known forms of batteries were called "Baghdad batteries" and were discovered in Mesopotamia (present-day Iraq) in the 1930s. These batteries, dating back to around 200 BC, were composed of a clay jar, an iron rod, and a copper cylinder. When filled with an electrolyte solution, such as vinegar or wine, the device could generate a small amount of electricity. The exact purpose of these batteries is still unknown, but some historians speculate that they may have been used for electroplating or medical treatments.

Another early form of battery was the Voltaic pile, invented by Italian physicist Alessandro Volta in 1800. The Voltaic pile consisted of alternating discs of copper and zinc, separated by pieces of cardboard soaked in an electrolyte solution. When a wire was connected between the top and bottom of the pile, a small electric current was generated. Volta's invention was the first true battery, as it could generate a continuous flow of electricity.

Volta's invention inspired a flurry of experimentation with batteries, and many inventors attempted to improve upon his design. One of the most successful was John Daniell, a British chemist who invented the Daniell cell in 1836. The Daniell cell was an improved version of the Voltaic pile, using a copper sulfate electrolyte and a zinc electrode. The Daniell cell was much more reliable than previous batteries and was widely used in telegraph systems and other early electrical applications.

In the late 19th century, the development of the lead-acid battery revolutionized the use of batteries for transportation. The lead-acid battery was invented by French physicist Gaston Planté in 1859 and consisted of two lead plates immersed in a sulfuric acid electrolyte. The lead-acid battery was the first rechargeable battery, and it quickly became popular for use in early electric vehicles and other portable applications.

In the early 20th century, new types of batteries were developed, including the nickel-iron battery and the nickel-cadmium battery. The nickel-iron battery, also known as the Edison battery, was invented by Thomas Edison in 1901 and used an alkaline electrolyte instead of acid. The nickel-cadmium battery, invented by Swedish scientist Waldemar Jungner in 1899, used a nickel oxide hydroxide cathode and a cadmium anode.

During World War II, the demand for batteries increased dramatically, leading to further innovations in battery technology. The development of the lithium-ion battery in the 1980s was a major breakthrough, as it allowed for much higher energy densities and longer cycle life than previous battery types. The lithium-ion battery is now the most common type of battery used in portable electronics, such as smartphones and laptops.

In recent years, there has been a growing interest in developing new types of batteries to meet the needs of emerging technologies such as electric vehicles and renewable energy storage. One promising technology is the solid-state battery, which uses a solid electrolyte instead of a liquid one, potentially offering higher energy densities and improved safety. Other research is focused on developing batteries using materials such as sodium or magnesium, which are more abundant and less expensive than lithium.

33 SEAT BELTS

The invention of the seat belt dates to the early 1900s when automobiles were first introduced. However, the modern seat belt that we are familiar with today was not introduced until much later.

In 1885, the first automobile was invented by Karl Benz. At that time, automobiles were considered a luxury item, and safety was not a top priority. It wasn't until the 1930s that safety concerns began to emerge. In 1930, the first safety belt was invented by George Cayley. However, this safety belt was not designed for cars but rather for airplanes. The safety belt was designed to keep pilots in their seats during turbulence or a crash.

In 1950, the first modern three-point seat belt was invented by Nils Bohlin, a Swedish engineer who was working for Volvo. The three-point seat belt was designed to restrain both the upper and lower body, providing maximum protection in the event of a crash. The three-point seat belt quickly became popular and was adopted by many car manufacturers around the world.

Despite the effectiveness of the three-point seat belt, it wasn't until the 1960s that seat belts became a standard feature in cars. In 1968, the United States government mandated that all new cars be equipped with seat belts. This was a major step forward for automobile safety, as seat belts had been proven to reduce the risk of death or injury in the event of a crash.

In the 1970s, there was a push to increase seat belt usage. Many people were still not using seat belts, and this was leading to a high number of fatalities on the road. In response to this, the government launched a campaign to increase seat belt usage. This campaign was successful, and by the 1980s, most people were wearing seat belts.

Over the years, seat belts have continued to evolve. In the 1980s, seat belt pretensioners were introduced. Pretensioners tighten the seat belt during a crash, reducing the amount of slack in the belt and increasing the effectiveness of the belt. In the 1990s, seat belt force limiters were introduced. Force limiters reduce the force of the seat belt during a crash, which helps to reduce the risk of injury.

In recent years, new technologies have been introduced to make seat belts even safer. In 2011, Ford introduced inflatable seat belts. Inflatable seat belts work by inflating like an airbag during a crash. This helps to distribute the force of the impact over a larger area, reducing the risk of injury.

Despite the many advancements in seat belt technology, there are still many people who do not wear seat belts. According to the National Highway Traffic Safety Administration, in 2019, 9,466 people were killed in crashes in which they were not wearing a seat belt. This represents 47% of all passenger vehicle occupants killed in crashes.

34 TAPE RECORDERS

The history of tape recorders dates to the early 20th century when the first practical magnetic recording was developed in Germany. It was the result of the work of a Danish engineer, Valdemar Poulsen, who created the Telegraphone, which used a thin steel wire as a recording medium. This early form of magnetic recording paved the way for the development of the tape recorder, which was to become one of the most important inventions of the 20th century.

In 1928, Fritz Pfleumer, a German engineer, developed the first magnetic tape. He coated a long strip of paper with magnetic particles and wound it around a spool. This magnetic tape was a significant improvement over the steel wire that was previously used because it was much thinner and could record higher-quality sound. The magnetic tape also allowed for longer recordings, which was a crucial development for the music industry.

The first tape recorder, called the Magnetophon, was developed in 1935 by the German company AEG. The Magnetophon used a magnetic tape to record and playback sound. The machine was large and expensive, making it primarily used for broadcasting and recording studios. The Magnetophon was revolutionary because it offered a higher quality of recording and playback than previous recording technologies.

During World War II, the tape recorder became an essential tool for intelligence agencies. They used tape recorders to record conversations and broadcasts and to analyze the language and communication of the enemy. The tape recorder was instrumental in the war effort, as it provided valuable intelligence that helped turn the tide of the war.

After the war, the tape recorder became more widely available to the general public. In 1948, the American company Ampex introduced the first commercially available tape recorder, the Model 200. The Model 200 was significant because it was the first recorder that used high-quality magnetic tape and could record and play back sound on multiple tracks.

In the 1950s, the tape recorder became a popular consumer product. The introduction of the compact cassette in 1963 further fueled the popularity of the tape recorder. The cassette was smaller, more portable, and less expensive than previous tape recorders, making it accessible to more people.

In the 1970s, the cassette tape became the dominant format for music distribution. The cassette was more durable and portable than vinyl records, and it was easier to manufacture and distribute. The introduction of the Sony Walkman in 1979 further popularized the cassette, as people could listen to music on the go.

In the 1980s, digital recording technology became available, and the Compact Disc (CD) was introduced in 1982. CDs offered superior sound quality and durability over cassette tapes, which led to a decline in the popularity of the tape recorder.

Despite the decline in popularity of the tape recorder, it remains an essential tool for many industries. The tape recorder is still used in professional recording studios and broadcasting, and it is a crucial tool for archivists and historians.

In recent years, there has been a resurgence in the popularity of the cassette tape. Some music enthusiasts prefer the sound quality of cassettes over digital formats, and many independent artists release their music on cassette to stand out from the crowd.

35 TEFLON

Teflon is a brand name for a synthetic fluoropolymer of tetrafluoroethylene, a thermoplastic material that is renowned for its non-stick and heat-resistant properties. It was first discovered in the late 1930s by a chemist named Roy Plunkett, who was working for the DuPont Company in the United States. Over the years, Teflon has become one of the most popular and widely used materials in various industries such as food packaging, cookware, and aerospace.

The discovery of Teflon was an accidental one. In 1938, Roy Plunkett was working on a project to create a new refrigerant gas. He had filled a cylinder with tetrafluoroethylene gas and left it outside overnight. When he returned the next day, he found that the gas had polymerized into a white, waxy substance that had unusual properties. Plunkett realized that he had stumbled upon something significant and began studying the properties of this new material.

The first patent for Teflon was filed in 1941 by the DuPont Company, and the company began producing the material on an industrial scale. Initially, Teflon was used as a coating for valves and pipes in the chemical industry due to its non-stick and corrosion-resistant properties. However, it wasn't until the 1950s that Teflon became popular in the consumer market.

In 1954, the first Teflon-coated frying pan was introduced by the French engineer Marc Grégoire. He had discovered the non-stick properties of Teflon when he accidentally spilled the material on his fishing gear, which made it easier to clean. Grégoire realized that Teflon could be used to create a non-stick coating for cookware, and he founded the Tefal Company to produce Teflon-coated frying pans.

The introduction of Teflon-coated cookware revolutionized the way people cooked food. The non-stick properties of Teflon made it possible to cook with less oil and fat, and cleaning up was much easier. Teflon-coated cookware became popular in the United States in the 1960s and 1970s, and it remains popular to this day.

In addition to its use in cookware, Teflon has also found its way into various other industries. It is used as a coating for non-stick food packaging such as microwave popcorn bags, as well as in the aerospace industry for its heat-resistant properties. Teflon is also used in the production of fabrics and textiles due to its water-repellent properties.

However, Teflon has not been without its controversies. In the early 2000s, concerns were raised about the safety of Teflon-coated cookware. It was discovered that the manufacturing process of Teflon involved the use of a chemical called perfluorooctanoic acid (PFOA), which was found to be toxic and carcinogenic. PFOA was also found to be present in Teflon-coated cookware and could potentially leach into food.

As a result of these concerns, the DuPont Company and other manufacturers began phasing out the use of PFOA in the manufacturing process of Teflon. The new Teflon products are now PFOA-free, and manufacturers have assured consumers that they are safe to use.

36 THE TELEVISION

The television is one of the most influential inventions of the 20th century, transforming the way people consume entertainment and information. It has its roots in the early 20th century, when inventors and scientists around the world were working on developing ways to transmit and display images over long distances.

One of the first people to make significant progress in this area was Scottish inventor John Logie Baird. In 1925, he successfully transmitted the first television image, a simple outline of a cross, over 10 feet. He continued to develop his technology, and in 1926 he demonstrated the first television set that could display moving images.

Baird's early television sets used a mechanical scanning system, which involved spinning a disk with holes in it in front of a light source. As the disk spun, the light would shine through the holes and onto a photoelectric cell, which would convert the light into an electrical signal. This signal could then be transmitted over wires or radio waves to a receiver, which would convert it back into a moving image.

While Baird's technology was groundbreaking, it was also limited by the low resolution and poor image quality of the mechanical scanning system. In the United States, a team of researchers led by Philo Farnsworth were working on a different approach to television, using electronic scanning instead.

Farnsworth's system used a cathode ray tube (CRT) to display the image, with an electron beam scanning back and forth across the screen to create the picture. His system was more efficient and produced higher-quality images than Baird's, and it quickly became the standard for television technology in the United States.

The first public demonstration of electronic television took place in San Francisco in 1927, and by the early 1930s, television sets were available for purchase in the United States. However, the technology was still expensive and not widely adopted, and it wasn't until after World War II that television became a truly mass-market product.

The post-war years saw explosive growth in the television industry, with millions of sets sold and networks springing up to broadcast programming to a growing audience. The 1950s and 60s were the golden age of television, with iconic shows like I Love Lucy, The Honeymooners, and The Ed Sullivan Show capturing the hearts of millions of viewers.

In the 1960s and 70s, color television became the norm, and programming expanded to include news, sports, and a wide range of entertainment options. The introduction of cable and satellite television in the 1980s and 90s further increased the number of channels and options available to viewers.

Today, television is omnipresent in homes around the world, and the industry continues to evolve and adapt to changing technologies and consumer preferences. From the early days of mechanical scanning to the high-definition, internet-connected sets of today, the history of television is a testament to human ingenuity and the power of innovation to shape our world.

37 ARTIFICIAL SNOW

Artificial snow is a technology that has been around for decades, and it has been instrumental in many industries, from winter sports to moviemaking. Its history dates to the early 20th century, where it was first developed in the United States.

The first recorded instance of artificial snow was in 1929, when a man named Frank Wells used a machine that he had built to create snow for a Christmas pageant in Hollywood, California. This machine used a combination of compressed air and water to create the snow, and it was an immediate success.

Following this success, other companies began to develop their own machines for creating artificial snow. One of the most significant of these was the Snow Engineering Corporation, which was founded in 1930 by Clarence Birdseye, the inventor of frozen food.

Snow Engineering Corporation created a machine that used a fan and water spray to create snow, which was then collected and stored in large tanks. The snow could then be transported to ski resorts and other locations where it was needed. This technology was a significant improvement over earlier methods, which involved crushing ice and then blowing it through a fan to create snow.

During the 1930s and 1940s, artificial snow became increasingly popular, and it was used in a variety of applications. In the film industry, it was used to create snow for movies set in winter environments, such as "Gone with the Wind" and "It's a Wonderful Life." In sports, it was used to create snow for ski slopes and other winter sports venues.

However, the development of artificial snow technology was not without its challenges. One of the biggest problems was finding the right combination of water and air to create snow that was both realistic and long-lasting. This required a lot of experimentation, and many early attempts at artificial snow were not very successful.

Another challenge was finding ways to store and transport the snow. Since it was made of water, it had to be kept cold to prevent it from melting. This meant that it had to be stored in refrigerated tanks and transported in refrigerated trucks.

Despite these challenges, artificial snow technology continued to evolve. In the 1950s and 1960s, new machines were developed that used different methods to create snow. One of the most significant of these was the "snow gun," which used compressed air and water to create snow that was similar in texture to natural snow.

Snow guns were first developed in the early 1950s, and they quickly became popular in the ski industry. They were used to create snow for ski slopes, and they were also used in ski parks and other winter sports venues.

Today, artificial snow technology is widely used in many different industries. In the film industry, it is used to create snow for movies and television shows. In sports, it is used to create snow for ski slopes, snowboarding parks, and other winter sports venues.

Artificial snow is also used in the tourism industry, where it is used to create snow in places where it does not naturally occur. For example, some ski resorts in warmer climates use artificial snow to create snow for their slopes.

In recent years, there has been increasing concern about the environmental impact of artificial snow. Critics argue that the process of creating artificial snow uses a lot of energy and water, and that it can have negative impacts on local ecosystems.

To address these concerns, some companies have begun to develop more sustainable methods of creating artificial snow. For example, some snow guns now use less water and energy, and some companies are experimenting with using alternative materials to create snow.

Despite these challenges, artificial snow technology continues to be an important tool in many industries. As technology continues to evolve, it is likely that we will see even more advances in the field of artificial snow.

DID YOU KNOW?

The pencil eraser was first added to the end of pencils in the 18th century after a mistake by an Italian scientist.

The rubber band was patented in 1845, but its real breakthrough came when it was used to bundle newspapers.

The common umbrella dates back over 4,000 years to ancient civilizations in Egypt and China.

The world's first traffic light was installed in 1868 in London, but it exploded less than a month later.

The design of the modern clothes hanger can be traced back to a wire factory worker in 1869.

The concept of Toilet Paper dates to ancient China, where it was first mass produced in thew 14th century.

The invention of the match in the 19th century rendered the practice of rubbing two sticks together obsolete.

The can opener was not invented until 1858, nearly 50 years after the invention of canned food.

The invention of the Refrigerator in the early 20th century revolutionized food storage and preservation.

The first wristwatch was created in 1812 by Abraham-Louis Breguet for the Queen of Naples.

The concept of the alarm clock can be traced back to ancient Greece, where they used water clocks with a pebble dropping system.

The rubber eraser was created by accident in the 18th century when an inventor mixed latex and sulfur.

38 THE SUPER SOAKER

The Super Soaker is a water gun that has been popular among children and adults alike for decades. It was invented by Lonnie Johnson, an engineer who was working for NASA at the time.

The story of the Super Soaker began in the early 1980s when Lonnie Johnson was working on a heat pump that used water instead of Freon. During his experiments, he noticed that the high-pressure stream of water coming from the nozzle of his device could be used for recreational purposes.

Inspired by this observation, Johnson began working on a prototype of a water gun that would use a similar mechanism to shoot a powerful stream of water. After several years of experimentation, he finally created a working prototype in 1989.

The first Super Soaker was called the Power Drencher and was sold under the Larami brand name. It was a simple device that used a pump to build up pressure in a reservoir of water. When the trigger was pulled, the pressure was released, and a stream of water was ejected from the nozzle.

The Power Drencher was an instant hit, and it quickly became one of the best-selling toys of the summer of 1990. However, Johnson was not content with just one successful product. He continued to improve on his design and came up with several new models over the years.

In 1991, Johnson introduced the Super Soaker 30, which was a smaller and more affordable version of the original. It was a huge success, and it paved the way for even more innovative designs in the years to come.

One of the most popular Super Soaker models of all time is the Super Soaker 50, which was introduced in 1992. It was larger than its predecessors and had a longer range, thanks to its improved pump mechanism. The Super Soaker 50 was a massive success, and it cemented the Super Soaker's place as one of the most beloved toys of all time.

Over the years, Johnson continued to innovate and improve on his design. In 1996, he introduced the Super Soaker CPS 2000, which was the first Super Soaker to use a pressurized reservoir system. This allowed for even more powerful streams of water, and it made the Super Soaker even more popular among children and adults alike.

Despite the success of the Super Soaker, Johnson faced several challenges along the way. One of the biggest challenges was finding a company that was willing to manufacture and distribute his product. He eventually partnered with the toy company Hasbro, which helped to take the Super Soaker to the next level.

Another challenge that Johnson faced was patent infringement. Several companies attempted to copy his design and sell their own version of the Super Soaker. However, Johnson fought back and won several legal battles to protect his invention.

Today, the Super Soaker remains one of the most popular toys of all time. It has been featured in countless movies and TV shows, and it has become a staple of summertime fun for generations of children.

In addition to its popularity as a toy, the Super Soaker has also had a significant impact on the world of science and engineering. Johnson's invention was a testament to the power of innovation and the importance of creativity and experimentation in the field of engineering.

In 2015, Johnson was inducted into the National Inventors Hall of Fame for his contributions to the world of engineering and his invention of the Super Soaker.

39 CHOCOLATE MILK

Chocolate milk, a popular beverage that combines milk and cocoa powder or chocolate syrup, has a history that dates back centuries. The origins of chocolate milk can be traced back to the ancient civilizations of the Aztecs and Mayans, who consumed a bitter beverage made from cocoa beans. However, the sweet, creamy beverage that we know today as chocolate milk is a relatively recent invention.

The first known recipe for chocolate milk was published in the late 17th century by Sir Hans Sloane, a British physician and naturalist. Sloane had traveled to Jamaica, where he observed the local people drinking a beverage made from cocoa beans mixed with water and spices. He found the beverage unpalatable and decided to mix the cocoa with milk instead. Sloane's recipe, which was included in his book "A Voyage to the Islands Madera, Barbados, Nieves, S. Christophers and Jamaica," called for a mixture of grated chocolate, milk, and sugar.

In the 18th and 19th centuries, chocolate milk became a popular drink in Europe, particularly in France and Spain. Chocolate was still relatively expensive at the time, so chocolate milk was considered a luxury beverage that was enjoyed mainly by the wealthy. However, the invention of milk chocolate in the 19th century made chocolate more widely available, and chocolate milk became a more affordable and accessible drink.

In the United States, chocolate milk first appeared in the early 1900s. In 1917, a Swiss immigrant named Walter Lowsky started selling a chocolate milk mix called Bosco, which became wildly popular. Bosco was originally marketed as a health drink and was even used as a source of nutrition for soldiers during World War II. After the war, Bosco continued to be a popular beverage for children, and its slogan, "I love Bosco," became a cultural touchstone.

In the 1950s and 1960s, chocolate milk became a staple in American school cafeterias. Milk was seen as an important source of calcium and other nutrients, and adding chocolate syrup was a way to make it more appealing to children. In fact, chocolate milk became so popular in schools that some parents and health advocates began to express concerns about its high sugar content. However, in recent years, studies have shown that chocolate milk can be a healthy beverage option for children, particularly athletes who need the extra energy and nutrients provided by the sugar and milk.

Today, chocolate milk is a beverage that is enjoyed by people of all ages all over the world. It is available in a variety of forms, including pre-packaged bottles, powder mixes, and syrup, and can be found in grocery stores, restaurants, and cafes. Many people enjoy chocolate milk as a treat, while others drink it for its nutritional benefits. In fact, chocolate milk is often recommended as a post-workout recovery drink due to its high protein and carbohydrate content.

While the origins of chocolate milk may be humble, its evolution into a beloved and versatile beverage is a testament to human creativity and ingenuity. From the Aztecs and Mayans to Sir Hans Sloane to Walter Lowsky and beyond, people have been experimenting with chocolate and milk for centuries, and the result is a drink that is both delicious and nutritious. Whether enjoyed as a nostalgic childhood treat or a post-workout recovery drink, chocolate milk is sure to remain a beloved beverage for years to come.

40 BASEBALL MITTS

Baseball mitts, also known as gloves, have been an integral part of the sport of baseball for over a century. They have evolved significantly since their inception, from simple leather gloves to highly specialized equipment designed to meet the needs of modern players.

The origins of baseball mitts can be traced back to the mid-19th century, when baseball was first starting to gain popularity in the United States. In those early days, players did not wear gloves, instead using their bare hands to catch the ball. This was a dangerous and often painful practice, as the ball was made of hard leather and could be thrown at speeds of up to 90 miles per hour.

The first gloves were designed to protect the fingers and palms of the players from injury. These gloves were made of leather and were little more than thin pads that were worn on the hands. They provided minimal protection but were better than nothing, and many players began to use them.

As the sport continued to grow, so did the gloves. In the late 1800s, players began to use larger, more padded gloves that were designed specifically for catching. These gloves were still made of leather, but they were thicker and more durable than earlier models. They had webbing between the thumb and forefinger, which allowed players to catch the ball more easily.

In the early 1900s, the first specialized catcher's mitt was introduced. This glove was larger and more heavily padded than other gloves, with a deep pocket that was designed to make it easier to catch fast pitches. Catcher's mitts are still used today and are among the most important pieces of equipment for any catcher.

In the 1920s and 1930s, gloves continued to evolve. Players began to use gloves with larger pockets and more padding, and the webbing between the thumb and forefinger became more elaborate. This allowed players to make more complex catches and to handle the ball more easily.

During World War II, there was a shortage of leather, and many gloves were made from other materials, such as canvas and nylon. These gloves were not as durable as leather gloves and did not offer as much protection, but they were better than nothing.

After the war, gloves began to evolve again. In the 1950s, gloves with more elaborate webbing patterns were introduced, allowing players to make more complex catches. The gloves also became more specialized, with different gloves designed for different positions. For example, first basemen's gloves had a larger, more rounded shape to make it easier to catch balls thrown from the infield.

In the 1960s and 1970s, gloves continued to evolve. Manufacturers began to experiment with new materials, such as synthetic leather and synthetic materials. These materials were lighter and more durable than leather, and they offered better protection against the impact of the ball. Some players even began to use gloves with built-in shock absorbers to help reduce the impact of catching fast pitches.

In the 1980s and 1990s, gloves became even more specialized. Pitcher's gloves, for example, were designed to be lighter and more flexible, allowing pitchers to grip the ball more easily. Infielders' gloves were smaller and more maneuverable, allowing infielders to make quick catches and throws.

Today, baseball gloves continue to evolve. Manufacturers are constantly experimenting with new materials and designs to create gloves that offer better protection, comfort, and performance. Many gloves now feature advanced technology, such as moisture-wicking fabrics and antimicrobial treatments, to help keep players cool and comfortable on the field.

41 THE MICROSCOPE

The microscope is an instrument that allows for the observation of objects and organisms that are too small to be seen with the naked eye. The history of the microscope dates to the late 16th century, when inventors began experimenting with various lenses and light sources to magnify small objects.

The earliest known microscope was created by Dutch spectacle maker Zacharias Janssen in the late 1590s. Janssen is credited with inventing the compound microscope, which used two lenses to magnify an object. This microscope was primitive and had a limited magnification power, but it was a significant breakthrough in the field of microscopy.

In the early 1600s, Galileo Galilei began experimenting with lenses and created a simple microscope that used a single convex lens to magnify objects. This microscope was not as powerful as Janssen's compound microscope, but it was portable and easy to use.

The next significant advancement in the history of the microscope came in 1665, when English scientist Robert Hooke published his book Micrographia. In this book, Hooke described his observations of various objects under a microscope, including insects, plants, and even the structure of cork. Hooke's book was widely popular and helped to spark interest in the field of microscopy.

In the 1670s, Dutch scientist Antonie van Leeuwenhoek made significant advancements in the field of microscopy by improving the quality of lenses and increasing the magnification power of microscopes. Van Leeuwenhoek's microscopes were small and used a single lens, but they were able to achieve much higher magnification than previous microscopes. Using his microscope, van Leeuwenhoek was able to observe single-celled organisms, which he called "animalcules."

In the 18th century, improvements in lens grinding and polishing techniques led to further advancements in the field of microscopy. Microscopes became more powerful and easier to use, and they were used for a variety of purposes, including medical research, botany, and zoology.

One of the most significant advancements in the history of the microscope came in the early 19th century with the development of the compound microscope. The compound microscope uses multiple lenses to magnify an object, and it allowed for much higher magnification than previous microscopes. This microscope was widely used in scientific research and helped to further our understanding of the microscopic world.

In the mid-19th century, German physicist Ernst Abbe made significant contributions to the field of microscopy by developing a mathematical theory that explained the limitations of microscope lenses. Abbe's theory, known as Abbe's diffraction limit, explained why microscopes could not achieve unlimited magnification and helped scientists to understand the limitations of the technology.

In the late 19th and early 20th centuries, advances in technology and manufacturing led to the development of new types of microscopes, including the electron microscope and the fluorescence microscope. The electron microscope uses beams of electrons to produce high-resolution images of objects, while the fluorescence microscope uses fluorescence to highlight specific structures within an object.

Today, microscopes are used in a wide range of fields, including biology, medicine, materials science, and nanotechnology. They have become essential tools for scientific research and have helped to advance our understanding of the microscopic world.

42 COFFEE CUP SLEEVES

Coffee cup sleeves, also known as coffee sleeves or coffee cozies, are a relatively recent addition to the coffee drinking experience. The history of coffee cup sleeves can be traced back to the early 1990s, when a woman named Jay Sorensen was traveling on a plane and received a cup of coffee that was too hot to hold.

Sorensen, a coffee shop owner from Portland, Oregon, decided to create a solution to the problem of hot coffee cups. He experimented with different materials and designs before coming up with a corrugated paper sleeve that could be slipped over the cup to insulate the heat and protect the hands.

Sorensen began selling his invention, which he called the "Java Jacket," to other coffee shops in the Portland area. The concept quickly caught on, and by the mid-1990s, coffee sleeves were being used by coffee shops across the United States.

The popularity of coffee sleeves continued to grow throughout the 1990s and early 2000s. In 2005, Starbucks introduced their own version of the coffee sleeve, called the "Starbucks Sleeve." The company distributed millions of these sleeves to its stores, further increasing the popularity of the concept.

Today, coffee sleeves are a common sight in coffee shops around the world. They are often made from recycled materials and are available in a variety of designs and colors. In addition to protecting hands from hot coffee cups, they also serve as a marketing tool for coffee shops and other businesses, with many companies printing their logos or other promotional messages on the sleeves.

43 THE SMILEY FACE

The Smiley Face is an iconic symbol that has become synonymous with happiness, positivity, and goodwill. It is a simple design consisting of a yellow circle, two black dots for eyes, and a black arc for a smile. Despite its apparent simplicity, the Smiley Face has a history that spans several decades and involves many different people and cultures.

The origins of the Smiley Face can be traced back to the 1960s, a time of great social and cultural change in America. During this period, many young people began to rebel against the established order and embrace new forms of expression and creativity. One of the most popular symbols of this counterculture was the "Have a Nice Day" slogan, which appeared on everything from t-shirts and bumper stickers to posters and buttons.

In 1963, a commercial artist named Harvey Ball was hired by a local insurance company in Worcester, Massachusetts, to create a design for a morale-boosting campaign. Ball quickly sketched out a simple smiley face with a yellow background, two black dots for eyes, and a black arc for a mouth. The design was intended to convey a sense of warmth, friendliness, and positivity, and it was an instant hit with the employees.

However, it wasn't until 1971 that the Smiley Face became a cultural phenomenon. That year, two brothers named Bernard and Murray Spain came up with the idea of printing the Smiley Face on buttons and selling them as a form of self-expression. The brothers, who were based in Philadelphia, began to market the buttons aggressively, and they quickly became a huge success. Within a few months, the Smiley Face had become a symbol of the counterculture, appearing on everything from t-shirts and hats to posters and greeting cards.

The popularity of the Smiley Face continued to grow throughout the 1970s, as more and more people embraced its message of positivity and goodwill. The design was adapted in various ways, with different colors, sizes, and styles appearing on a wide range of products. In 1972, the song "Smiling Faces Sometimes" by The Undisputed Truth became a hit, further cementing the Smiley Face's place in popular culture.

Despite its enormous success, the Smiley Face began to fade from public consciousness in the 1980s, as the counterculture gave way to more mainstream forms of expression. However, it experienced a resurgence in the 1990s, when the design was adopted by the rave culture and became a symbol of the electronic dance music scene. The Smiley Face was used on flyers, posters, and t-shirts, and it was often associated with the use of MDMA, a popular party drug.

Today, the Smiley Face continues to be an enduring symbol of happiness, positivity, and goodwill. It is used by a wide range of people and organizations, from corporations and charities to individuals and activists. The design has been adapted in many ways, with variations appearing in different colors, shapes, and styles.

One of the most interesting aspects of the Smiley Face's history is its global appeal. Despite its origins in America, the design has been embraced by people all over the world and has become a truly international symbol of positivity and happiness. It has been adapted in many different cultures, with variations appearing in different languages, scripts, and visual styles.

For example, in Japan, the Smiley Face is known as "Emoji," and it is used extensively in digital communication. The Japanese version of the Smiley Face is slightly different from the original design, with a more rounded shape and slightly tilted eyes. In China, the Smiley Face is known as "Kaomoji," and it is used in text messages, social media, and other digital platforms.

44 BENDY STRAWS

Bendy straws are a staple of American culture, and their history is a testament to the ingenuity and creativity of human beings. Over the years, they have been used for everything from sipping drinks to crafting art projects, and their simple design has become an iconic symbol of childhood nostalgia.

The first bendy straws were invented by Joseph Friedman in the 1930s. Friedman, who was a father of three young children, noticed that his kids had a difficult time drinking through straight straws. They would often spill their drinks or struggle to get the last bit of liquid out of the bottom of the glass. To solve this problem, he inserted a screw into a straight straw and wrapped dental floss around it. He then removed the screw, leaving a series of ridges that made it easier for his children to bend the straw to their desired angle.

Friedman patented his invention in 1937 and began selling it under the name "Flex-Straw." His initial production run was a success, but he quickly ran into manufacturing difficulties. The process of creating the ridges in the straw was labor-intensive, and the materials he used were prone to breaking. Friedman continued to refine his design, experimenting with different materials and manufacturing methods.

It wasn't until the 1940s that bendy straws began to gain widespread popularity. This was due in part to the war effort, which led to a shortage of metal straws. Bendy straws, which were made from plastic, were a convenient and affordable alternative. They quickly caught on in restaurants, where they were used to serve drinks to customers.

In the decades that followed, bendy straws became a fixture in American culture. They were used in everything from fast food restaurants to schools to hospitals. They were even featured in movies and TV shows, where they became a symbol of childhood innocence and playfulness.

Over time, the design of bendy straws has evolved. Today, they are typically made from a combination of polypropylene and polyethylene, which makes them more durable and flexible than earlier models. They also come in a variety of colors and sizes, making them a popular choice for party favors and other special events.

Despite their popularity, bendy straws have come under fire in recent years for their environmental impact. They are difficult to recycle and can end up in landfills or oceans, where they can harm wildlife. As a result, many companies and individuals are looking for alternatives to traditional plastic straws. Some are turning to biodegradable materials like paper or bamboo, while others are opting for reusable straws made from stainless steel or silicone.

Despite the challenges they face, bendy straws remain a beloved symbol of American culture. They have played an important role in our history, providing a simple and effective solution to a common problem. Whether they are being used to drink a milkshake or to create a work of art, bendy straws will always hold a special place in our hearts.

45 THE SMARTWATCH

The Smartwatch is a modern-day accessory that combines the functionality of a wristwatch with the features of a smartphone. Smartwatches have come a long way from the bulky, limited devices they were when first introduced. Today, they are sleek, intuitive, and offer a variety of features that enhance their usefulness and appeal.

The history of the Smartwatch can be traced back to the early 1980s when the first wristwatch computer, the Pulsar Calculator Watch, was introduced. However, it wasn't until the 1990s that companies like Seiko and Timex introduced the first digital watches with built-in computer functions, such as calculators and calendars. These early digital watches were the predecessors to the modern-day Smartwatch.

The first true Smartwatch was the Seiko Ruputer, which was released in 1998. It featured a monochrome LCD screen and could be connected to a computer via a serial port. The Ruputer had a variety of features, including a calendar, calculator, and email capabilities. However, it was bulky and expensive, which made it unappealing to the average consumer.

In 2000, Microsoft introduced its Smart Personal Object Technology (SPOT) platform, which enabled watches to receive information wirelessly. This technology allowed users to receive news, weather, and stock information directly on their watches. However, the watches were expensive, and the technology was not widely adopted.

In 2004, Fossil introduced the Wrist PDA, which was a more compact version of the Seiko Ruputer. The Wrist PDA had a touch screen and could be synced with a computer to transfer data. However, like its predecessors, it was expensive and had limited functionality.

In 2007, Apple introduced the iPhone, which changed the game for mobile technology. As smartphones became more popular, the idea of a Smartwatch became more feasible. In 2010, Apple released the first generation of the iPod Nano, which could be worn as a watch with third-party accessories. This sparked a trend of DIY Smartwatches that were created by attaching a small computer to a wristband.

In 2012, Pebble Technology launched a Kickstarter campaign for its Smartwatch, which raised over $10 million. The Pebble Smartwatch was compatible with both iOS and Android devices and had a long battery life. The watch could display notifications, control music, and had fitness tracking capabilities. Pebble paved the way for other companies, such as Samsung and LG, to enter the Smartwatch market.

In 2014, Apple released its first Smartwatch, the Apple Watch. The Apple Watch was a game-changer for the Smartwatch industry. It was sleek, intuitive, and had a variety of features, including fitness tracking, messaging, and phone calls. The watch could also be used to control other Apple devices, such as the iPhone and Apple TV. The release of the Apple Watch sparked a surge in the popularity of Smartwatches and led to increased competition in the market.

Since the release of the Apple Watch, Smartwatches have continued to evolve and improve. They are now more intuitive, have longer battery life, and offer a wider range of features. Smartwatches are no longer just an accessory for tech enthusiasts but have become a mainstream product that appeals to a broad range of consumers.

46 GAS MASKS

Gas masks have become a symbol of war and disaster, but their history is much more extensive than most people realize. From their origins in the trenches of World War I to their modern use in the face of global pandemics, gas masks have played a vital role in protecting people from deadly gases, fumes, and airborne particles.

The early history of gas masks can be traced back to the 1800s when scientists began experimenting with various methods of protecting themselves from toxic fumes and gases. The first documented use of a rudimentary gas mask dates to 1847 when Scottish chemist James B. Neilson designed a respirator to protect coal miners from carbon monoxide.

However, it wasn't until the outbreak of World War I in 1914 that gas masks truly came into their own. During the early months of the war, both sides relied heavily on poisonous gas as a weapon, causing widespread panic and devastation. Soldiers were forced to wear crude masks made from cotton pads soaked in chemicals or rags dipped in urine to protect themselves.

It wasn't until 1915 that British chemist Edward Harrison developed the first practical gas mask, which used activated charcoal to filter out poisonous gasses. The mask, known as the "Harrison respirator," was quickly adopted by the British military and was a significant improvement over earlier designs. However, it was still far from perfect, and soldiers often suffered from eye irritation, skin rashes, and other problems.

In response to these issues, a team of British scientists led by Frederick Guthrie developed a new gas mask that used a combination of activated charcoal and granulated soda lime to filter out harmful gasses. This mask, known as the "Black Veil Respirator," was much more effective than earlier designs and was quickly adopted by the British military.

Meanwhile, in Germany, chemist Fritz Haber was also working on developing a gas mask that could protect soldiers from poison gas. Haber, who had played a key role in the development of chlorine gas as a weapon, was motivated by a desire to protect German soldiers from the same weapon he had helped to create. In 1915, Haber's team developed a mask that used a mixture of activated charcoal and sodium thiosulfate to filter out chlorine gas.

Throughout the rest of the war, both sides continued to develop and improve their gas masks, and by the end of the conflict, gas masks had become a standard piece of military equipment. The use of poisonous gas as a weapon had also become less effective as a result of the widespread adoption of gas masks and other protective measures.

In the years following World War I, gas masks continued to evolve and improve. In the 1920s and 1930s, new materials such as rubber and plastic were used to create more durable and effective masks. In 1934, the British military introduced the "Light Anti-Gas Respirator" (L.A.R.), which was designed to protect soldiers from all types of poisonous gas.

The outbreak of World War II in 1939 once again brought gas masks to the forefront of military technology. The masks used during this conflict were even more advanced than those of World War I, incorporating new features such as voice amplifiers and improved filtration systems.

In addition to their military use, gas masks also became an important tool for civilians during World War II. In the United Kingdom, for example, millions of gas masks were distributed to the general population as part of the government's air raid precautions.

After World War II, gas masks continued to be used by military forces around the world, but they also found new applications in civilian life. In the 1950s and 1960s, gas masks were commonly used by workers in industries such as mining, firefighting, and chemical production.

47 THE VACUUM CLEANER

The vacuum cleaner is a household appliance that has become a useful tool in the modern world. It has revolutionized cleaning and made it much easier and more efficient. While the modern vacuum cleaner is an electric device, the concept of cleaning using suction power has been around for centuries.

The earliest known reference to a vacuum cleaner-like device dates to the mid-16th century, when an English inventor named Thomas Duster created a machine that used bellows to create a suction effect. However, it wasn't until the 19th century that the idea of a mechanical vacuum cleaner began to take shape.

The first mechanical vacuum cleaner was patented by American inventor Daniel Hess in 1860. Hess's machine consisted of hand-cranked bellows that created a suction effect, which was used to pick up dirt and dust. However, the machine was bulky, expensive, and impractical, and it failed to gain widespread popularity.

It wasn't until 1901 that the first electric vacuum cleaner was invented. Hubert Cecil Booth, a British engineer, designed a machine that used an electric motor to create suction. Booth's machine was far more practical and efficient than Hess's, and it soon became popular in Europe.

It wasn't long before the electric vacuum cleaner made its way across the Atlantic to America. In 1907, James Murray Spangler, a janitor from Ohio, invented the first portable electric vacuum cleaner. Spangler's machine was small, lightweight, and easy to maneuver, making it much more practical than earlier vacuum cleaners.

Spangler's design was a success, and he began selling his vacuum cleaners to friends and neighbors. However, he lacked the capital to manufacture the machines on a large scale, so he sold his patent to a relative, William Hoover.

Hoover saw the potential in Spangler's invention and began manufacturing the machines on a large scale. He improved the design and added features such as a detachable hose and a dust bag, which made the machines even more practical and efficient.

Hoover's vacuum cleaners quickly became popular in America, and the Hoover brand became synonymous with vacuum cleaners. Other companies soon followed suit, and the vacuum cleaner became a common household appliance in America and Europe.

The basic design of the vacuum cleaner remained largely unchanged for several decades, but in the mid-20th century, new technologies and materials led to significant improvements in vacuum cleaner design.

One of the most significant developments was the invention of the cyclonic vacuum cleaner by James Dyson in the 1980s. Dyson's machine used centrifugal force to separate dirt and dust from the air, eliminating the need for a dust bag. The cyclonic vacuum cleaner was more efficient, powerful, and durable than earlier designs, and it quickly gained popularity.

In recent years, robotic vacuum cleaners have become increasingly popular. These machines use sensors and software to navigate around a room and clean it automatically. While they are not as powerful as traditional vacuum cleaners, they are convenient and require little effort on the part of the user.

48 THE ABSENTEE BALLOT

The absentee ballot, also known as the mail-in ballot or postal vote, is a form of voting that allows registered voters to cast their ballots remotely, without being physically present at a polling station. While the use of absentee ballots has become increasingly common in recent years, the history of this form of voting dates back centuries.

The first recorded instance of absentee voting can be traced back to the 17th century, when French soldiers serving overseas were permitted to cast their ballots by proxy in national elections. However, it wasn't until the American Civil War that absentee voting began to gain widespread use.

During the Civil War, soldiers on both sides of the conflict were given the opportunity to cast absentee ballots. The Union Army made a concerted effort to ensure that soldiers had the ability to vote, as it was believed that giving soldiers the right to vote would encourage greater support for the war effort. In 1864, Congress passed the Soldier Voting Act, which allowed soldiers in the field to vote by absentee ballot in federal elections.

Following the Civil War, absentee voting became more widespread, particularly in states with large populations of military personnel. However, it wasn't until the 20th century that absentee voting truly became a common practice. In 1924, the state of Pennsylvania became the first state to permit absentee voting without requiring an excuse. By the 1950s, most states had followed suit, and absentee voting became a regular part of the American electoral process.

Over the years, the use of absentee voting has continued to expand, with many states now offering early voting and no-excuse absentee voting. In recent years, the use of absentee ballots has become a topic of intense debate, with some arguing that it is necessary to ensure that all eligible voters could cast their ballots, while others have expressed concerns about the potential for fraud.

One of the most significant developments in the history of absentee voting occurred in the wake of the September 11, 2001, terrorist attacks. In response to concerns about the safety of polling stations, Congress passed the Help America Vote Act of 2002, which provided funding to states to improve their voting systems and expand access to absentee voting.

The 2020 United States presidential election saw an unprecedented surge in the use of absentee ballots. With the COVID-19 pandemic still raging across the country, many voters were hesitant to risk exposure by voting in person. As a result, many states expanded their absentee voting systems and encouraged voters to cast their ballots by mail. This led to record-breaking numbers of absentee ballots being cast, with some states reporting that more than half of all votes were cast by mail.

While the use of absentee ballots has become more common in recent years, there are still concerns about the potential for fraud. In some cases, absentee ballots have been the subject of controversy, with allegations of ballot harvesting, voter fraud, and other irregularities. However, studies have shown that instances of voter fraud are extremely rare, and that the use of absentee ballots is generally safe and effective.

49 AIRPLANES

The history of airplanes is a tale of human ingenuity and innovation. It spans centuries and involves the contributions of countless individuals and organizations, each with their own unique story to tell.

The idea of flying has fascinated humans for thousands of years, with early attempts at flight dating back to ancient China, Greece, and Egypt. However, it wasn't until the 19th century that significant progress was made in the field of aviation.

In the 1800s, inventors began experimenting with balloons and gliders, attempting to achieve sustained flight. In 1852, Henri Giffard built the first successful powered airship, which used a steam engine to propel it through the air. While Giffard's airship was not capable of sustained flight, it marked an important step forward in aviation technology.

The first successful glider flight took place in 1853, when Englishman George Cayley built a glider that could carry a human passenger. Cayley's glider featured a fixed-wing design that would later become a key feature of modern airplanes.

In the late 1800s, the development of internal combustion engines sparked a new era of aviation innovation. Inventors such as Samuel Langley and the Wright brothers began experimenting with powered flight, with the Wright brothers achieving the first sustained, controlled flight in a powered airplane in 1903.

The early years of aviation were marked by rapid progress, as designers and engineers raced to improve airplane design and performance. In 1914,

World War I broke out, and airplanes quickly became an important tool of war. During the war, airplanes were used for reconnaissance, aerial combat, and bombing missions, leading to further advancements in aviation technology.

After the war, aviation continued to evolve and expand, with companies such as Boeing and Douglas becoming major players in the industry. In the 1920s and 1930s, air travel began to take off, as airlines began offering passenger flights across the globe. This era also saw the development of new airplane designs, including the monoplane, which replaced the biplane as the dominant design in aviation.

The 1940s marked another significant turning point in aviation history, with the outbreak of World War II leading to rapid advancements in airplane technology. The war saw the development of jet engines and the first supersonic flight, as well as the introduction of strategic bombers such as the B-29 and the Lancaster.

Following the war, commercial air travel continued to expand, with the development of larger, faster, and more efficient airplanes. In the 1950s, the introduction of jet airliners such as the Boeing 707 and the Douglas DC-8 revolutionized air travel, making it faster, safer, and more comfortable than ever before.

The 1960s marked another important milestone in aviation history, with the first manned spaceflight taking place in 1961. This era also saw the development of new airplane designs, such as the jumbo jet and the supersonic Concorde.

In the decades that followed, aviation continued to evolve, with advances in technology and materials leading to the development of more fuel-efficient and environmentally friendly airplanes. The rise of low-cost airlines and the growth of air travel in emerging markets such as Asia and the Middle East have also helped to reshape the industry.

Today, airplanes play a vital role in global transportation, connecting people and goods across the world. While the history of airplanes is a long and complex one, it is a testament to human ingenuity and the power of innovation to shape the world around us.

50 ELECTRICITY

From ancient times, humans have been aware of the existence of electricity in the form of lightning and static electricity, but it was not until the 19th century that electricity became a practical source of power that could be used for lighting, heating, and powering machines.

The early history of electricity can be traced back to the ancient Greeks, who were the first to observe the effects of static electricity. They discovered that rubbing certain materials together, such as amber and fur, would produce an electrical charge that could attract small objects like feathers or bits of straw. This phenomenon was named "elektron" after the Greek word for amber.

In the centuries that followed, the study of electricity was largely theoretical, with little practical application. It was not until the 17th century that scientists began to make significant breakthroughs in the understanding of electricity. In 1600, the English physician William Gilbert published a book titled "De Magnete," which explored the properties of magnets and the relationship between magnetism and electricity.

In the 18th century, experiments with electricity began to become more practical. Benjamin Franklin, one of the most famous figures in the history of electricity, conducted a series of experiments in the mid-18th century that demonstrated the connection between lightning and electricity. He famously flew a kite during a thunderstorm, proving that lightning was a form of electricity.

In the early 19th century, scientists began to develop ways to generate electricity on a large scale. In 1800, Alessandro Volta invented the first battery, which produced a steady flow of electricity. This was a breakthrough, as it allowed scientists to conduct experiments with electricity in a more controlled environment.

In the decades that followed, scientists developed several new technologies for generating electricity. In 1821, Michael Faraday invented the electric motor, which used the principle of electromagnetic induction to convert electrical energy into mechanical energy. This was a crucial development, as it allowed electricity to be used to power machines.

The mid-19th century saw a flurry of activity in the field of electricity. In 1831, Faraday discovered electromagnetic induction, which allowed for the generation of electricity using a rotating magnet and a stationary wire coil. This principle formed the basis for the development of the dynamo, a device that could convert mechanical energy into electrical energy.

In 1879, Thomas Edison invented the first practical incandescent light bulb, which used a carbon filament to produce light when an electric current was passed through it. This was a breakthrough, as it allowed electricity to be used for lighting on a large scale.

The late 19th century saw the rapid expansion of the electrical industry, as electricity began to be used to power factories, streetlights, and homes. The development of the alternating current (AC) system by Nikola Tesla in the 1880s made it possible to transmit electricity over long distances, which allowed for the creation of large-scale power plants.

The early 20th century saw further developments in the field of electricity, as new technologies were developed for generating and distributing electricity. In the 1920s, the first hydroelectric power plants were built, harnessing the power of water to generate electricity. In the 1930s, the first nuclear power plants were developed, using the power of the atom to generate electricity.

Today, electricity is an important part of modern life, powering everything from smartphones to cities. The development of renewable energy sources such as wind and solar power is reducing our dependence on fossil fuels and paving the way for a more sustainable future.

51 CELL PHONES

Cell phones, or mobile phones, have revolutionized the way people communicate with each other. The ability to make phone calls and send messages on the go has made cell phones an indispensable part of modern life. The history of cell phones is a story of innovation and development, from the early days of bulky and expensive devices to the sleek and powerful smartphones of today.

The first mobile phone was invented in 1973 by Martin Cooper, a researcher at Motorola. The device was large and heavy, weighing over two pounds, and was nicknamed the "brick" due to its size and shape. It had limited functionality and could only make phone calls, but it was a breakthrough in mobile technology. The first commercial cell phone was introduced in 1983 by Motorola, and it was called the DynaTAC 8000X. It cost $3,995 and was only available in the United States.

Throughout the 1980s and early 1990s, cell phones became smaller, more affordable, and more widely available. In 1989, the first flip phone, the Motorola StarTAC, was released, and it quickly became a popular choice among consumers. The 1990s saw the introduction of the first GSM network, which allowed for global roaming and paved the way for international cell phone use. Nokia became the dominant cell phone manufacturer during this time, and its 5110 model was a best-seller.

The late 1990s and early 2000s saw the rise of the smartphone. In 1999, the first smartphone, the Nokia 9210 Communicator, was released. It had a color screen, could send and receive email, and had a full keyboard. However, it was expensive and did not sell well. The BlackBerry, which was released in 2002, was the first smartphone to gain widespread popularity. It was designed for business users and had a full keyboard for easy typing.

In 2007, Apple released the iPhone, which revolutionized the smartphone industry. It had a touchscreen interface, could access the internet, and had a wide range of apps available for download. The iPhone was an instant success, and it paved the way for other companies to develop their own smartphones. Samsung, HTC, and Google all entered the smartphone market in the years following the iPhone's release.

Today, smartphones are an essential part of everyday life for millions of people around the world. They are used for everything from communication and entertainment to productivity and shopping. The latest smartphones are incredibly powerful and can do things that were once thought impossible on a mobile device. They have become so integral to modern life that many people would be lost without them.

However, the rise of cell phones and smartphones has not been without controversy. Some people believe that they are addictive and that they can have negative effects on mental health. Others are concerned about the impact that they are having on society, including the rise of cyberbullying and the spread of misinformation online. As cell phones continue to evolve and become more advanced, it is likely that these debates will continue.

52 GOOGLE

Google is undoubtedly one of the most significant companies in the world, and it has become a household name for its search engine that provides quick and accurate results. Today, Google has expanded its services to include email, cloud storage, video streaming, and much more. The company's success story is fascinating and can be traced back to its humble beginnings in 1995.

The story of Google begins with two computer science students at Stanford University, Larry Page and Sergey Brin. Both were working on their Ph.D. research projects when they met and started working together. In 1995, Larry Page had been exploring the idea of ranking web pages based on the number of links pointing to them. He believed that this approach would produce more relevant search results. This concept later became the basis of Google's PageRank algorithm.

Initially, Page and Brin called their search engine "Backrub," but in 1997 they changed the name to "Google," a play on the word "googol," which is a mathematical term for the number one followed by 100 zeros. The name was chosen to reflect the vast amount of information that the search engine would be able to index.

In 1998, Google launched its search engine on the internet, and it quickly gained popularity due to its simple and clean interface and accurate search results. Google's PageRank algorithm was a significant factor in the success of its search engine, as it allowed Google to deliver more relevant search results than its competitors.

The success of the search engine prompted Page and Brin to establish Google as a company in September 1998. They set up their first office in a garage in Menlo Park, California, and started hiring employees. In 1999, Google secured its first investment of $100,000 from Andy Bechtolsheim, a co-founder of Sun Microsystems. With this investment, Google was able to purchase its first server equipment and expand its team.

As Google continued to grow, it attracted the attention of venture capitalists, and in 2000, the company raised $25 million in funding from investors, including Sequoia Capital and Kleiner Perkins. With this investment, Google was able to expand its operations and open offices in New York City and Tokyo.

In 2001, Google launched AdWords, an advertising program that allowed businesses to place targeted ads on Google's search results pages. AdWords quickly became a significant source of revenue for the company and helped Google become one of the most profitable companies in the world.

In 2004, Google went public with an initial public offering (IPO) that raised $1.67 billion. The IPO made many of Google's employees and early investors millionaires and helped the company raise funds for future expansion.

Over the years, Google has continued to innovate and expand its services. In 2005, it acquired the company behind Google Maps and started offering its own mapping service. In 2006, Google acquired YouTube, the world's largest video-sharing platform. In 2008, Google launched its own web browser, Google Chrome, which quickly became one of the most popular browsers in the world.

In 2015, Google restructured itself and became a subsidiary of Alphabet Inc., a holding company that owns several other companies, including Waymo, Calico, and Verily. Larry Page became the CEO of Alphabet, and Sundar Pichai became the CEO of Google.

Today, Google is one of the most valuable companies in the world, with a market capitalization of over $1 trillion. Its search engine is used by billions of people every day, and its other services, such as Gmail, Google Drive, and Google Photos, are widely used and highly regarded.

53 FIDGET SPINNERS

Fidget spinners became a sensation in 2017, with people of all ages twirling them in their hands. The devices are made of a central bearing and two or three prongs that rotate around it. However, the history of fidget spinners goes back much further than that.

The idea of a spinning device to help with concentration and anxiety dates to ancient times. In ancient Greece, people used a small toy called a "triacontaeter" that was similar in design to the modern fidget spinner. It had 30 sides, and people would spin it on a table or on their fingers.

In the 1990s, Catherine Hettinger, an inventor from Florida, came up with a similar device that she called the "spinning toy." Hettinger was suffering from myasthenia gravis, a disease that causes muscle weakness, and she created the toy to help her daughter cope with her own anxiety. Hettinger eventually patented the spinning toy in 1997, but she couldn't find a manufacturer to produce it.

The spinning toy went largely unnoticed for nearly two decades until 2016 when a small company called Zuru Toys discovered Hettinger's patent and began manufacturing the devices. The company marketed them to help with stress and anxiety, and the toys quickly became popular among children and adults alike.

The fidget spinner craze started in early 2017 when a few schools in the United States began banning them, claiming that they were a distraction in the classroom. The bans sparked a wave of media attention, and suddenly fidget spinners were everywhere. They were sold in stores, online, and on street corners. People started customizing their spinners with different colors and designs, and manufacturers began producing spinners with lights and sound effects.

The popularity of fidget spinners was not without controversy, however. Some experts claimed that there was no scientific evidence to support the idea that they helped with anxiety or concentration. Others criticized the devices as a distraction and a fad that would soon pass.

Despite the controversy, fidget spinners remained popular throughout 2017. They were sold in all kinds of stores, from toy stores to convenience stores, and people continued to spin them in public places. Some people even started using fidget spinners as a form of meditation or mindfulness practice.

By the end of 2017, the fidget spinner craze had begun to die down. Sales of the devices had dropped, and some stores had stopped carrying them altogether. However, fidget spinners remain a popular toy and stress reliever, and they continue to be sold online and in some stores.

54 THE INTERNET

The internet is an indispensable part of modern society, connecting billions of people around the world to a wealth of information and resources. Its history can be traced back to the mid-20th century, when scientists and engineers began exploring ways to connect computers and share information across networks.

The origins of the internet can be traced back to the early 1960s, when the US Department of Defense began funding research into computer networking. At the time, computers were large, expensive, and mainly used by government and academic institutions. The goal was to create a system that could link these disparate machines together and allow researchers to share data and resources more efficiently.

The first breakthrough in this effort came in the form of the Advanced Research Projects Agency Network (ARPANET), which was created in 1969. ARPANET was a decentralized network of computers that used packet switching technology to transmit data across the network. This allowed information to be broken down into small packets and sent to its destination via multiple routes, making the network more robust and less prone to failure.

ARPANET initially connected just four nodes, located at research institutions in California and Utah. However, it quickly grew as more institutions joined the network and began sharing data and resources. By the mid-1970s, ARPANET had become a key tool for researchers in a wide range of fields.

The next major milestone in the development of the internet came in

1983, when ARPANET was split into two separate networks: ARPANET and the Defense Data Network (DDN). The DDN was specifically designed to support military communications, while ARPANET continued to be used for research purposes.

At the same time, a new networking protocol called TCP/IP (Transmission Control Protocol/Internet Protocol) was developed to standardize how data was transmitted across networks. TCP/IP was designed to be flexible, reliable, and scalable, making it ideal for the rapidly growing internet.

By the late 1980s, the internet had begun to expand beyond its original roots in the academic and research communities. This was largely due to the development of the World Wide Web (WWW) by British computer scientist Tim Berners-Lee. The WWW was a system of interconnected hypertext documents that could be accessed via the internet using a web browser.

The first website was created in 1991, and by the mid-1990s, the internet had become a commercial phenomenon, with businesses and consumers alike using it to buy and sell goods, access information, and communicate with each other.

As the internet grew, new technologies and services emerged to support its continued expansion. In the mid-1990s, search engines like Yahoo! and Google were created to help users find information online, while online marketplaces like Amazon and eBay made it easy for consumers to buy and sell goods online.

The early 2000s saw the rise of social media platforms like MySpace and Facebook, which allowed users to create profiles, connect with friends and family, and share content with each other. At the same time, broadband internet connections became more widely available, making it possible to stream audio and video content online.

Today, the internet is an essential part of modern life, connecting people around the world to a wealth of information, entertainment, and resources. From online shopping and banking to social media and streaming video, the internet has transformed the way we live, work, and communicate with each other. And as new technologies like artificial intelligence, blockchain, and the Internet of Things continue to emerge, the internet is sure to play an even more central role in shaping our future.

55 THE TELEPHONE

The telephone is a device used for transmitting sound over long distances using electrical signals. It revolutionized communication by allowing people to talk to each other even if they were miles apart. The history of the telephone is full of interesting stories and characters who contributed to its development.

The roots of the telephone can be traced back to the early 19th century when inventors were experimenting with ways to transmit sound over wires. One of the earliest devices was the telegraph, which used electrical signals to transmit messages over long distances. In 1837, a young inventor named Samuel Morse created the first practical telegraph, which became widely used throughout the United States and Europe.

However, the telegraph was limited in its ability to transmit sound. Messages had to be translated into code, and the sound of the message could not be transmitted. This limitation was a significant problem for many people who wanted to communicate with each other more easily.

In the late 1860s, two inventors independently began working on a solution to this problem.
Alexander Graham Bell and Elisha Gray both developed devices that could transmit sound over wires. Bell's device, which he called the "telegraphophone," used a membrane to convert sound waves into electrical signals that could be transmitted over a wire. Gray's device, which he called the "harmonic telegraph," used a series of tuned reeds to transmit sound.

Both inventors filed patents for their devices in 1876. However, Bell's device became the most famous and widely used, and he is generally credited with inventing the telephone. On March 10, 1876, Bell made the first successful transmission of speech over his device, saying, "Mr. Watson, come here, I want to see you." This historic moment is considered the birth of the telephone.

Bell's invention quickly spread throughout the world, and within a few years, telephones were in use in many cities and towns. The first telephone exchange was established in New Haven, Connecticut, in 1878. This exchange allowed multiple telephones to be connected to a central switchboard, making it possible for people to call each other without having to manually connect the wires.

In the years that followed, many improvements were made to the telephone. In 1889, Almon Strowger invented the first automatic telephone exchange, which eliminated the need for operators to manually connect calls. Instead, calls were automatically routed through a mechanical switchboard. This invention was a significant step forward in the development of the telephone.

In the early 20th century, telephones became more widely used, and telephone companies began to emerge. These companies were responsible for building and maintaining the telephone networks that connected people around the world. The most famous of these companies was the Bell Telephone Company, which was founded by Alexander Graham Bell and his associates.

In the 1920s and 1930s, new technologies were developed that improved the telephone even further. The introduction of rotary dialing allowed people to make calls more quickly and efficiently, and the development of long-distance lines made it possible for people to call each other across the country and even around the world.

During World War II, the telephone became an essential tool for communication between military leaders and troops. The development of mobile phones in the 1970s made it possible for people to communicate while on the go, and the introduction of digital technology in the 1980s and 1990s made it possible for phones to do much more than just make calls.

Today, the telephone has evolved into a multifunctional device that can be used for a wide variety of tasks. Smartphones allow people to make calls, send messages, take pictures, surf the web, and use a wide variety of apps.

56 BIKINIS

The bikini is a type of swimsuit that has become popular around the world for its revealing design. The garment typically consists of two separate pieces – a top and a bottom – that are worn by women at beaches, pools, and other outdoor locations during the summer months. Although the bikini may seem like a relatively modern invention, its history can be traced back to ancient civilizations.

The bikini is named after Bikini Atoll, a Pacific Ocean Island that was used by the United States military as a site for nuclear testing in the mid-1940s. The swimsuit was introduced to the world on July 5, 1946, by French fashion designer Louis Réard, who named it after the atoll. The bikini was a radical departure from the modest swimwear that was popular at the time, and it caused a sensation when it was first unveiled.

However, the bikini was not the first two-piece swimsuit. In fact, women had been wearing two-piece swimsuits since the 1920s, when they began to reject the restrictive clothing of the Victorian era. These early two-piece swimsuits were known as "beach pajamas" and consisted of a top that covered the torso and shorts that covered the legs. However, they still provided more coverage than the modern bikini, and they were not widely accepted until the 1930s.

In the years leading up to World War II, swimsuits continued to become more revealing. By the 1940s, many women were wearing swimsuits that consisted of a bra-like top and shorts or a skirt. However, these swimsuits were still relatively modest compared to the bikini.

The bikini was initially met with resistance from the fashion industry and many members of the public, who felt that it was too revealing and immodest. In fact, Réard had to hire a stripper to model the bikini at its debut because no respectable model would wear it. However, the bikini quickly gained popularity among younger women who wanted to rebel against traditional standards of modesty.

In the 1950s, the bikini became even more popular thanks to Hollywood stars such as Brigitte Bardot and Marilyn Monroe. These actresses were often photographed wearing bikinis, which helped to popularize the swimsuit and make it more acceptable to the general public.

During the 1960s, the bikini continued to evolve. The "monokini" was introduced in 1964, which was a one-piece swimsuit that had the sides cut out to expose the midriff. The monokini was even more daring than the bikini, and it caused a sensation when it was first introduced.

In the 1970s, the bikini became even more popular as women's liberation movements gained momentum. The swimsuit was seen as a symbol of freedom and women's rights, and it was worn by women of all ages and sizes.

In the decades since the bikini was first introduced, it has continued to evolve and change. Today, there are many different styles of bikinis available, from string bikinis that barely cover anything to more modest designs that provide more coverage.

Despite its controversial beginnings, the bikini has become a staple of summer fashion and a symbol of women's liberation. Its evolution over the years reflects changing attitudes towards gender, sexuality, and modesty. While the bikini may continue to change and evolve in the future, it is likely that it will always be a popular and iconic part of women's fashion.

57 FOAM FINGERS

Foam fingers are an accessory seen in sporting events and rallies around the world. These oversized hands, usually made of foam or other lightweight materials, have become a staple of sports culture and a symbol of fan enthusiasm. While the exact origins of the foam finger are difficult to trace, it is widely believed that the foam finger has its roots in American sports culture and has evolved over the years to become the iconic symbol we know today.

One of the earliest references to a foam finger can be traced back to the 1971 college football season. Steve Novak, a student at the University of Washington, was looking for a way to show support for his team during the annual rivalry game against the University of Oregon. He came up with the idea of creating a large foam finger, which he painted purple and gold to match his school's colors. The finger featured the number one, which was meant to signify that the University of Washington was the top team in the country. Novak brought his creation to the game, and it was an instant hit with fans, who began asking where they could get their own.

From there, the popularity of foam fingers began to grow. In the early 1980s, a company called Spirit Industries began producing foam fingers for sports teams and events across the United States. Spirit Industries was founded by Geral Fauss, who had been making custom foam products since the 1960s. Fauss saw the potential in foam fingers as a marketing tool for sports teams and began producing them in large quantities. Over the years, Spirit Industries became one of the leading manufacturers of foam fingers and other promotional products in the United States.

The foam finger's popularity really took off in the 1980s and 1990s. As sports teams began to understand the marketing potential of foam fingers, they began commissioning their own designs. The New York Mets, for example, commissioned a foam finger with the team's logo on it for their 1986 World Series run. The finger quickly became a hit with fans and has since become a beloved symbol of the team's success.

The foam finger's popularity also extended beyond sports. In 1985, a foam finger made an appearance in the music video for the hit song "We Are the World." The finger, which was painted with the American flag, was held up by Michael Jackson and other members of the song's chorus during the recording of the video. This moment helped to cement the foam finger's place in American popular culture.

Over the years, foam fingers have continued to evolve. While the basic design of the finger has remained the same, manufacturers have introduced new features to make the fingers more interactive and engaging for fans. Some foam fingers, for example, now feature built-in noisemakers or other accessories that can be used to show support for a team or player.

Today, foam fingers are a regular sight at sporting events and rallies around the world. They are a symbol of fan enthusiasm and a way for people to show support for their favorite teams and players. While the history of the foam finger is not well documented, this iconic accessory has played an important role in American sports culture and popular culture more broadly. Whether you're a die-hard sports fan or simply looking to show your support for a cause, there's nothing quite like waving a foam finger in the air and letting everyone know where your loyalties lie.

58 METAL DETECTORS

Metal detectors are devices that use electromagnetic fields to detect the presence of metal objects in the vicinity. They have been used for a variety of purposes, including locating buried artifacts, finding lost or discarded items, and detecting weapons or contraband. The history of metal detectors dates to the early 20th century, when scientists first began to experiment with the use of electromagnetic waves for various applications.

The first metal detector was invented by Alexander Graham Bell in 1881. Bell was working on a device to help locate bullets in President James Garfield's body after he was shot by an assassin. Although the device was unsuccessful in finding the bullets, it did lead to the development of the first metal detector.

In 1925, Gerhard Fischer, a German immigrant living in the United States, invented the first practical metal detector. Fischer's invention used a radio-frequency oscillator to detect metal objects underground. The device was simple but effective, and it quickly became popular among treasure hunters and archaeologists.

During World War II, metal detectors were used by the military to locate mines and other explosive devices. The devices were also used by civilians to locate unexploded bombs and other dangerous objects in areas that had been bombed.

In the 1950s, metal detectors became more widely available to the public. Hobbyists and treasure hunters began using metal detectors to search for lost or buried items, such as coins, jewelry, and other artifacts. In 1954, White's Electronics, a company founded by Kenneth White, began producing metal detectors for hobbyists.

In the 1960s and 1970s, metal detectors became even more popular among hobbyists and treasure hunters. This was due in part to the availability of inexpensive metal detectors, which made it easier for people to get started in the hobby. During this time, many metal detector clubs were formed, and competitions were held to see who could find the most valuable or interesting items.

In the 1980s and 1990s, metal detectors continued to evolve. The development of microprocessors and digital signal processing allowed for more advanced metal detectors that were able to discriminate between different types of metals and ignore unwanted signals. This made it easier for treasure hunters to locate valuable items while filtering out junk signals.

Today, metal detectors are used for a variety of purposes, including treasure hunting, archaeological research, security screening, and industrial applications. Some metal detectors are even used in medical applications, such as locating metal fragments in a patient's body.

In recent years, metal detector technology has continued to evolve. Advances in signal processing and data analysis have led to more accurate and sensitive metal detectors that can detect smaller and deeper targets. Some metal detectors are even equipped with GPS technology, which allows users to map the locations of their finds and share them with other enthusiasts.

59 VOLLEYBALL

Volleyball is a popular team sport played by millions of people around the world. It is a game that involves two teams of six players each, who try to score points by hitting a ball over a net and into the opponent's court. The history of volleyball dates to the late 19th century, when it was invented by William G. Morgan, a physical education director at the YMCA in Holyoke, Massachusetts.

In the early days, volleyball was known as "Mintonette," and it was played with a basketball net and a rubber ball. The objective of the game was to keep the ball in the air without letting it touch the ground. The first official game of volleyball was played on July 7, 1896, at Springfield College in Massachusetts.

The game of volleyball quickly gained popularity in the United States, and in 1900, it was introduced to Canada. By 1907, the game had spread to other parts of the world, including Europe and Asia. Volleyball was included in the program of the Far Eastern Games in 1913, and it was played at the Olympics for the first time in 1964, in Tokyo, Japan.

Over the years, the rules of volleyball have undergone several changes, as the game evolved and became more competitive. In 1916, the game was changed from 21 points to 15 points per set. In 1920, the net height was raised to 2.43 meters for men and 2.24 meters for women. In 1947, the number of players per team was reduced from nine to six, and in 1957, the substitution rule was introduced.

The first international volleyball tournament was held in 1913, between the United States, Canada, and Japan. In 1949, the International Volleyball Federation (FIVB) was formed, and it became the governing body of the sport. Today, the FIVB has over 220 member nations, and it organizes several international tournaments, including the Volleyball World Cup, the Volleyball World Championship, and the Volleyball World Grand Prix.

Volleyball has become a popular sport around the world, with millions of people playing the game at the amateur and professional levels. It is played in schools, colleges, and universities, and it is a popular sport at the Olympics. In addition, there are several professional volleyball leagues around the world, including the Italian Serie A1, the Brazilian Superliga, and the Russian Volleyball Super League.

One of the most iconic moments in the history of volleyball came in 1984, when the United States men's team won the gold medal at the Olympics in Los Angeles. The team, which was coached by Doug Beal, included several talented players, including Karch Kiraly, Steve Timmons, and Craig Buck. The United States defeated Brazil in the final, to win their first Olympic gold medal in volleyball.

In recent years, volleyball has undergone several changes, as the game has become more fast-paced and exciting. The introduction of the Libero position in 1999, which allows a player to substitute for a defensive specialist without counting towards the team's substitution limit, has made the game more dynamic. In addition, the introduction of the rally point system, where a point is awarded to the team that wins each rally, has made the game more competitive and intense.

Today, volleyball is a sport that is enjoyed by people of all ages and backgrounds. It is a game that requires skill, speed, and agility, and it provides an excellent workout for the body. Whether playing for fun or at a competitive level, volleyball is a sport that brings people together and promotes teamwork, sportsmanship, and camaraderie.

60 THE MENORAH

The menorah is a Jewish symbol that has a long and rich history. The menorah is a seven-branched candelabrum, which has been used in Jewish worship for thousands of years. The menorah has become an important symbol of Jewish identity and has played a significant role in Jewish history.

The menorah's roots can be traced back to the biblical period. In the book of Exodus, God commanded Moses to construct a golden lampstand with seven branches to be used in the tabernacle. The tabernacle was a portable sanctuary used by the Israelites during their wanderings in the desert. The menorah was placed in the Holy Place of the tabernacle and was lit every day by the priests.

The menorah played an important role in the daily worship of the Israelites. It was a symbol of God's presence and served as a reminder of the covenant between God and the Israelites. The menorah also served as a symbol of the Israelites' mission to be a light to the nations.

After the Israelites settled in the land of Israel, the menorah was placed in the Temple in Jerusalem. The Temple was built by King Solomon and was the center of Jewish worship. The menorah remained in the Temple until its destruction by the Babylonians in 586 BCE.

After the Babylonian exile, the Jews returned to Jerusalem and rebuilt the Temple. The menorah was once again placed in the Temple and remained there until the Temple was destroyed by the Romans in 70 CE. The destruction of the Temple was a catastrophic event in Jewish history and had a profound impact on Jewish worship.

After the destruction of the Temple, the Jews were forced to adapt their worship practices. The menorah became an important symbol of Jewish identity and was used in synagogues as a reminder of the Temple. The seven-branched menorah became the official emblem of the State of Israel in 1949 and is still used as a symbol of Jewish identity today.

The menorah has played a significant role in Jewish history and has been used in many different contexts. During the Hanukkah holiday, a special nine-branched menorah called a Hanukkiah is used. The Hanukkah commemorates the miracle of the oil that occurred during the rededication of the Temple after it was desecrated by the Greeks.

According to tradition, the Jews only had enough oil to light the menorah for one day, but miraculously, the oil lasted for eight days. The Hanukkiah is lit each night of Hanukkah to commemorate this miracle.

The menorah has also been used in Jewish art and has been depicted in many different forms. The menorah has been carved in stone, painted on walls, and even used as a motif on coins. The menorah has also been used in modern Jewish art, and many artists have created their own interpretations of the menorah.

In addition to its use in Jewish worship, the menorah has also been used as a symbol of peace and unity. The menorah has been used in interfaith events to symbolize the shared values of different religions. The menorah has also been used as a symbol of hope and resilience in times of adversity.

61 GINGERBREAD

Gingerbread is a classic dessert that has been enjoyed by people all over the world for centuries. Its unique flavor and aroma have made it a popular treat during the holidays, but it can be enjoyed at any time of the year. The history of gingerbread is a long and fascinating one, spanning many centuries and cultures.

The earliest recorded gingerbread recipe dates to ancient Greece, where ginger was used as a medicinal herb. The ancient Greeks made gingerbread by mixing ginger, honey, and breadcrumbs together and baking them into a cake-like dessert. This recipe was later adopted by the Romans, who spread it throughout their empire.

In medieval Europe, gingerbread became a popular treat at fairs and markets. It was often shaped into figures and decorated with sugar and icing. The gingerbread man, one of the most iconic gingerbread shapes, is said to have been created by Queen Elizabeth I of England, who had gingerbread men made in the likeness of her courtiers.

During the Renaissance, gingerbread became a popular gift among royalty and nobility. It was often molded into intricate shapes, such as castles and animals, and decorated with gold leaf and other expensive materials. Gingerbread houses also became popular during this time, with people creating elaborate structures out of gingerbread, candy, and other sweets.

In the 16th century, gingerbread was brought to America by European settlers. The colonists adapted the recipe to include local ingredients such as molasses and maple syrup. Gingerbread was also popular among sailors, who believed that ginger helped to prevent sea sickness.

In the 19th century, gingerbread became a popular Christmas treat in Europe and America. It was often shaped into festive shapes, such as Christmas trees and stockings, and decorated with icing and other decorations. Gingerbread houses also became a popular Christmas tradition, with families creating their own edible houses to decorate and display during the holiday season.

Today, gingerbread is enjoyed all over the world in many different forms. In Germany, gingerbread is called Lebkuchen and is often shaped into hearts and decorated with icing. In Sweden, gingerbread is called Pepparkakor and is often served with mulled wine. In the United States, gingerbread is often served as a cake or cookie, and is a popular holiday treat.

62 CHRISTMAS ORNAMENTS

Christmas ornaments have been an integral part of holiday celebrations for centuries. These decorations add a touch of whimsy and magic to the season, and they have evolved in countless ways over the years. From simple homemade decorations to intricate, handcrafted works of art, Christmas ornaments have a history that spans centuries and continents.

The origins of Christmas ornaments can be traced back to ancient cultures, including the Egyptians and the Romans. These societies used decorative objects to celebrate the winter solstice, which marked the end of the harvest season and the beginning of winter. The Egyptians, for example, would hang ornaments made of palm fronds and other natural materials on their trees to symbolize the coming of spring.

In the 16th century, the German tradition of the Christmas tree began to take shape. These trees were decorated with candles, apples, and other items that represented the bounty of the harvest season. It was during this time that Christmas ornaments as we know them today began to emerge. Glassblowers in the town of Lauscha, Germany began crafting delicate glass ornaments in a variety of shapes and colors, including balls, stars, and figurines. These ornaments quickly became popular throughout Germany and beyond.

By the 1800s, the tradition of decorating Christmas trees with ornaments had spread throughout Europe and beyond. In America, German immigrants brought the tradition with them and popularized the use of Christmas ornaments in the United States. The first American-made Christmas ornaments were simple decorations made from popcorn, cranberries, and other natural materials. As the manufacturing industry grew, however, more elaborate and intricate ornaments became available.

In the late 1800s, F.W. Woolworth began importing glass ornaments from Germany to sell in his stores in the United States. These ornaments, which were highly detailed and handcrafted, were expensive and often reserved for the wealthy. However, as production methods improved, glass ornaments became more affordable and accessible to people of all classes.

In the early 1900s, the trend towards handmade ornaments began to emerge. Families began creating their own decorations using materials such as paper, felt, and even food. These ornaments were often simple and rustic in design, but they added a personal touch to holiday decorations.

During World War II, materials such as metal and glass were in short supply, and many families were unable to afford expensive decorations. As a result, homemade ornaments once again became popular. Families would make ornaments out of paper, tin, and other materials, often using recycled items.

As the post-war era began, the popularity of Christmas ornaments continued to grow. With the rise of mass production techniques, manufacturers were able to create a wide variety of ornaments at affordable prices. Today, Christmas ornaments come in a dizzying array of designs, materials, and styles, ranging from traditional glass baubles to whimsical figurines to high-tech LED lights.

Despite their many variations, Christmas ornaments remain an essential part of holiday traditions around the world. They bring joy and warmth to homes during the winter season, and they serve as a reminder of the importance of family, friends, and community. Whether they are handcrafted by artisans or mass-produced in factories, Christmas ornaments continue to inspire and delight people of all ages and backgrounds.

63 BABY CARRIAGES

Baby carriages, also known as baby strollers or prams, have been a popular mode of transportation for infants and young children for over two centuries. The design and features of these carriages have undergone significant changes over the years, reflecting the evolution of societal needs, technological advancements, and fashion trends.

The earliest baby carriages were not designed for convenience or comfort, but for the practical purpose of allowing parents to take their children outside while freeing up their hands to perform other tasks. These early models, which appeared in England in the early 1700s, were simply wooden boxes on wheels that were pushed by a caregiver. These "push chairs" were usually reserved for the wealthy, as they were expensive and required a staff member to push them.

In the early 1800s, the first modern-style baby carriage was introduced. This design featured a lightweight wicker basket with a folding hood that could be adjusted to protect the baby from the sun or rain. These carriages, called "perambulators" or "prams," quickly gained popularity and were soon being mass-produced for middle-class families. The design also incorporated suspension, making the ride smoother and more comfortable for the baby.

As the 19th century progressed, baby carriages became more elaborate, with ornate designs and additional features such as brakes, adjustable handles, and folding mechanisms for easier storage. The carriage became a status symbol, with manufacturers catering to the tastes of the upper classes with more luxurious and expensive models.

During the 20th century, baby carriages continued to evolve, with new materials such as steel, aluminum, and plastic being incorporated into the designs. The introduction of rubber tires and ball bearings in the early 1900s made the ride even smoother, and the addition of brakes and adjustable seats made the carriages safer and more comfortable for both the baby and the caregiver.

In the 1950s, the first umbrella strollers were introduced. These lightweight and compact designs could be folded and carried easily, making them ideal for travel and urban environments. This marked a significant shift away from the bulkier and more ornate designs of the past.

In the 1960s and 1970s, the rise of the feminist movement and the increasing number of women in the workforce led to a greater demand for baby strollers that were easier to manage and more practical. This led to the introduction of the first jogging strollers, which were designed to be more durable and easier to maneuver on rough terrain.

In recent years, baby strollers have become even more advanced, with features such as built-in speakers, smartphone docks, and self-propelling capabilities. The rise of sustainable and eco-friendly materials has also influenced the design of modern baby strollers, with manufacturers increasingly using materials such as bamboo and organic cotton.

The history of baby carriages has not been without controversy. In the early 1900s, concerns were raised about the safety of baby carriages, with reports of accidents and injuries caused by faulty designs. This led to the introduction of safety standards and regulations, and today, all baby strollers sold in the United States must meet safety standards set by the Consumer Product Safety Commission.

Despite these concerns, baby carriages have remained a popular mode of transportation for infants and young children, and their design and features continue to evolve to meet the changing needs of parents and caregivers. From the simple wooden boxes of the 18th century to the high-tech strollers of today, the history of baby carriages reflects the evolution of society and technology, and the enduring desire of parents to provide the best possible care for their children.

64 BLOOD BANKS

Blood banks are an integral part of modern healthcare, providing life-saving blood transfusions to those in need. The history of blood banks dates to the early 20th century and has evolved significantly over the years.

The concept of blood transfusions dates to ancient times, with early attempts to transfuse blood recorded as early as the 17th century. However, these early attempts were often unsuccessful and were associated with high mortality rates.

It was not until the early 20th century that blood transfusions became a more practical and successful medical procedure. In 1901, the Austrian physician Karl Landsteiner discovered the ABO blood group system, which allowed for the safe transfusion of blood between compatible blood types. This discovery was a breakthrough in the field of transfusion medicine and paved the way for the establishment of blood banks.

The first blood bank was established in 1937 by Dr. Bernard Fantus at the Cook County Hospital in Chicago, USA. The idea behind the blood bank was to collect and store blood from volunteer donors for use in transfusions. The success of the Cook County Hospital blood bank inspired the establishment of many other blood banks around the world.

During World War II, blood banks played a crucial role in the medical care of wounded soldiers. Blood was in high demand, and the establishment of mobile blood banks allowed for the rapid transport of blood to the front lines. This resulted in a significant decrease in mortality rates among wounded soldiers.

Following the war, blood banks continued to grow and evolve. In 1948, the American Association of Blood Banks was established, which set standards for blood banking and transfusion practices. The association also played a major role in the development of new blood products, such as plasma and platelets.

In the 1950s and 1960s, advancements in refrigeration and blood storage technology allowed for the safe long-term storage of blood. This made it possible to establish large-scale blood banks, which could provide a steady supply of blood for transfusions.

In the 1970s and 1980s, concerns emerged over the safety of blood transfusions. The spread of infectious diseases such as HIV and hepatitis through blood transfusions led to the development of strict screening procedures for blood donors. This included testing for infectious diseases and screening for high-risk behaviors.

Today, blood banks continue to play a crucial role in modern healthcare. The World Health Organization estimates that approximately 118.4 million blood donations are collected worldwide each year. Blood is used for a wide range of medical procedures, including surgeries, cancer treatments, and trauma care.

In addition to providing blood for transfusions, blood banks also play a role in medical research. Blood samples can be used to study the genetic basis of diseases and develop new treatments.

Blood banks have also been instrumental in disaster relief efforts. Following natural disasters or major accidents, blood banks can quickly mobilize to provide emergency blood supplies to those in need.

In recent years, advancements in technology have allowed for the development of new blood products, such as recombinant clotting factors and artificial blood substitutes. These products have the potential to revolutionize transfusion medicine and improve the safety and efficacy of blood transfusions.

65 ANTIBIOTICS

Antibiotics are one of the most important inventions in the history of medicine. They have saved countless lives by fighting bacterial infections and have revolutionized the way doctors treat infectious diseases. The discovery of antibiotics is a story of perseverance, scientific breakthroughs, and a race against time to save lives.

The history of antibiotics begins with the observation of the antimicrobial properties of certain substances. For example, ancient Egyptians used molds and other natural substances to treat infections. In the 19th century, scientists began to isolate and study these substances in the laboratory. In 1877, Louis Pasteur demonstrated that bacteria could be killed by exposure to heat, a process known as sterilization. This led to the development of heat sterilization techniques that are still used today to sterilize medical equipment and supplies.

In the early 20th century, researchers began to search for chemicals that could kill bacteria. One of the first successful antibiotics was discovered by Alexander Fleming in 1928. Fleming was a Scottish physician and bacteriologist who was studying the properties of the bacterium Staphylococcus aureus. He noticed that a mold called Penicillium notatum had contaminated one of his petri dishes and was killing the bacteria growing on it. He realized that the mold was producing a substance that was toxic to the bacteria and named it penicillin.

Despite Fleming's discovery, it was not until the 1940s that penicillin became widely used. This was due to the efforts of two researchers, Howard Florey and Ernst Chain, who developed a way to isolate and produce large quantities of penicillin. They collaborated with the pharmaceutical company

Pfizer to produce the drug on a large scale, and by the end of World War II, penicillin was being used to treat soldiers wounded on the battlefield.

The success of penicillin inspired other researchers to search for new antibiotics. In the 1940s and 1950s, many important antibiotics were discovered, including streptomycin, chloramphenicol, and tetracycline. These drugs were effective against a wide range of bacterial infections, and their discovery revolutionized the field of medicine.

However, the overuse and misuse of antibiotics have led to the development of antibiotic-resistant bacteria. When bacteria are exposed to antibiotics, some of them may survive and develop mutations that allow them to resist the effects of the drugs. These resistant bacteria can then spread and cause infections that are difficult or impossible to treat with existing antibiotics.

To combat antibiotic resistance, researchers have continued to search for new antibiotics and to develop strategies to prevent the spread of resistant bacteria. This includes the development of vaccines, the use of infection control measures in hospitals, and the development of new antibiotics that can target resistant bacteria.

In recent years, there have been some promising developments in the search for new antibiotics. For example, researchers have discovered new compounds that are effective against bacteria that are resistant to existing antibiotics. They have also developed new approaches to antibiotic development, such as using computer simulations to design drugs that can target specific bacterial proteins.

66 BRAILLE

Braille is a writing and reading system used by people who are visually impaired or blind. It consists of raised dots that can be felt by the fingers, and each dot or combination of dots represents a letter or other symbol. The system was developed in the early 19th century by Louis Braille, a Frenchman who lost his sight as a child. His invention revolutionized education and communication for people with visual impairments and has been used ever since.

The history of Braille dates to the early 19th century when Louis Braille was born in Coupvray, France, in 1809. As a young child, Braille accidentally injured his eye while playing with his father's tools, and the injury soon became infected, causing him to lose his sight completely. Despite this setback, Braille was a bright and curious child, and he was determined to learn and explore the world around him.

Braille's education began at a local school for the blind, where he learned to read using a system of raised letters that was popular at the time. However, this system had its limitations, as it was difficult to read complex texts and write down thoughts and ideas. Braille was not satisfied with this, and he began to experiment with other methods of writing and reading.

One day, Braille discovered a military code system used by soldiers to communicate in the dark without light. This system consisted of raised dots that could be felt by the fingers and was used to convey letters and numbers. Braille was fascinated by this code, and he set out to adapt it to create a system that could be used by blind people to read and write.

Braille spent several years developing his new writing and reading system. He experimented with different combinations of dots and symbols, testing them on his own fingertips to see which ones were easiest to read and distinguish. Finally, in 1824, Braille unveiled his new system to the world, and it was an immediate success.

The Braille system consisted of six dots arranged in two columns of three dots each. These dots could be raised or not raised, and each combination represented a different letter, number, or punctuation mark. The system was easy to learn and use, and it quickly spread throughout France and the world.

The success of the Braille system led to the establishment of new schools and institutions for the blind, where blind children and adults could receive an education and learn to read and write using the new system. Braille himself became a teacher at the Royal Institute for Blind Youth in Paris, where he taught the Braille system to a new generation of students.

Over time, the Braille system has evolved and improved, with new symbols and variations added to make it easier to read and write in different languages and contexts. Today, Braille is used all over the world, and it remains an essential tool for people with visual impairments who want to communicate, learn, and participate fully in society.

67 BRACES

Braces, also known as dental braces or orthodontic braces, are devices that are used to align and straighten teeth. The history of braces can be traced back to ancient times, when people used various methods to try and straighten their teeth.

In ancient Egypt, for example, people used catgut to tie their teeth together to straighten them. They also used metal wires to try and move teeth into the desired position. The ancient Greeks and Romans also tried to straighten teeth using various methods, including tying them together with gold wire.

The first true orthodontic braces, however, were developed in the 18th century by French dentist Pierre Fauchard. Fauchard is often referred to as the "father of modern dentistry" and is credited with many dental innovations, including the development of orthodontic braces.

Fauchard's braces were made of a flat strip of metal, which was placed over the teeth and then tied in place with thread. The strip of metal had slots cut into it, which allowed the dentist to adjust the position of the teeth as needed.

In the 19th century, another French dentist named Louis Bourdet developed a more advanced form of braces. Bourdet's braces consisted of a series of wires and springs that were attached to the teeth and used to move them into the desired position. Bourdet's braces were much more effective than Fauchard's and were used by dentists for many years.

In the early 20th century, several American dentists began to develop their own forms of braces. One of the most influential was Edward Angle, who is often referred to as the "father of modern orthodontics." Angle developed a system of braces that used brackets and wires to move the teeth into position. His system was much more precise than previous methods and is still used today in modified forms.

During the 20th century, braces became increasingly popular as more and more people became interested in improving the appearance of their teeth. In the 1970s and 1980s, the development of new materials, such as stainless steel and ceramics, led to the creation of braces that were much more comfortable and aesthetically pleasing than previous versions.

Today, there are many different types of braces available, including traditional metal braces, clear braces, lingual braces (which are placed on the inside of the teeth), and self-ligating braces (which do not require elastic bands). There are also newer technologies, such as Invisalign, which uses clear plastic aligners to straighten teeth.

In addition to traditional braces, there are also several other orthodontic devices that can be used to correct problems with the teeth and jaws. These include headgear, which is used to correct overbites and underbites, and expanders, which are used to widen the upper jaw.

While braces have come a long way since the ancient Egyptians were tying their teeth together with catgut, they continue to be an important tool in modern dentistry. Whether you're looking to improve your appearance, correct a bite problem, or simply improve the health of your teeth and gums, braces can help you achieve your goals.

68 PAPER TOWELS

Paper towels are an essential part of everyday life, and they are used for a wide range of purposes, including cleaning, drying hands, and wiping up spills. But where did this household item come from, and how did it become so popular?

The history of paper towels can be traced back to the early 1900s when they were first introduced as a disposable alternative to cloth towels. At that time, paper towels were primarily used in public restrooms and were marketed as a more hygienic option for drying hands. However, it wasn't until the 1930s that paper towels became widely available for home use.

The early paper towels were made from a type of tissue paper, which was absorbent but not very strong. This meant that they were not well-suited to heavy-duty cleaning tasks, and they tended to tear easily when wet. In the 1930s, however, a new type of paper towel was introduced that was much stronger and more absorbent. This new type of paper towel was made from a blend of wood pulp and cotton, which gave it greater strength and durability.

During World War II, paper towels became even more popular as they were used by the military for a variety of purposes, including cleaning equipment and wiping up spills. This increased demand for paper towels led to the development of new manufacturing techniques that allowed for faster production and lower costs.

In the post-war era, paper towels became a common household item, and they were used for a wide range of tasks. This was partly since they were more convenient than cloth towels, which had to be washed and dried after each use. Paper towels, on the other hand, could be simply thrown away after use, which made them a popular choice for busy households.

In the 1950s, the paper towel industry underwent a major transformation with the introduction of the first "roll" paper towel. This new type of paper towel was much more convenient than the old-style flat sheets, as it could be easily dispensed from a roll holder. This made it easier for consumers to use paper towels for a wider range of tasks, and it also led to increased sales for paper towel manufacturers.

Throughout the 1960s and 1970s, the popularity of paper towels continued to grow, as more and more consumers discovered their convenience and versatility. During this time, manufacturers introduced a wide range of different types of paper towels, including ones with greater absorbency and ones that were treated with special chemicals to make them stronger and more durable.

In the 1980s and 1990s, paper towels became even more pervasive, as they were used in a wide range of commercial and industrial settings. This was partly because they were more hygienic than cloth towels, which could harbor bacteria and other germs. Paper towels also became a popular choice for use in public restrooms, as they were seen as a more convenient and sanitary alternative to cloth towels.

Today, paper towels are an essential part of modern life, and they are used for a wide range of purposes, both in homes and in commercial settings. They are available in a wide range of different sizes, shapes, and styles, including perforated rolls, folded sheets, and single-use wipes. And while they are still primarily made from wood pulp, manufacturers have continued to innovate and develop new types of paper towels that are even stronger, more absorbent, and more eco-friendly.

In recent years, there has been growing concern about the environmental impact of paper towels, particularly as they are often used once and then thrown away. As a result, many consumers are now looking for more eco-friendly alternatives, such as reusable cloth towels or compostable paper towels made from recycled materials.

69 WRENCHES

Wrenches are one of the most essential tools used in mechanical and industrial work. The word wrench comes from the Old English word "wrencan," which means to twist or turn. The first wrenches were simple devices made from wood, which were used to grip and turn objects. Over time, the design and materials used to make wrenches have evolved, resulting in a wide range of wrenches for different applications.

The first wrenches were made in the Middle Ages, where they were primarily used in the construction of siege engines and machines. These early wrenches were made from wood, and they were used to tighten bolts and nuts. The wooden wrenches were not very effective, and they often broke due to the force required to turn bolts and nuts. This led to the development of iron wrenches, which were stronger and more durable.

The first iron wrenches were made in the 18th century. These early wrenches were made from wrought iron, and they were primarily used in the construction of steam engines and textile machines. The first mass-produced wrench was made by Solymon Merrick in 1835. Merrick's wrench was made from a single piece of iron, and it was designed to be used with square nuts. The design of the wrench was simple, but it was effective and efficient, and it quickly became popular among mechanics and machinists.

The adjustable wrench was invented in the 1840s by a man named Edwin Beard Budding. Budding was a British mechanic who had previously invented the lawnmower. The adjustable wrench was designed to be used with a wide range of bolt and nut sizes, and it quickly became a popular tool among mechanics and machinists. The first adjustable wrenches were made from steel, and they were manually adjusted using a screw mechanism.

In the late 19th century, a new type of wrench was developed called the socket wrench. The socket wrench was invented by J.J. Richardson in 1863, and it was designed to be used with hexagonal nuts and bolts. The socket wrench was more versatile than the adjustable wrench, and it allowed mechanics to work more quickly and efficiently. The first socket wrenches were made from steel, but later versions were made from chrome-plated steel and other materials.

During the 20th century, wrenches continued to evolve, and new designs were developed to meet the needs of different industries. In the 1920s, the torque wrench was invented. The torque wrench is a specialized wrench that is used to apply a specific amount of torque to a bolt or nut. This is important in industries such as aviation and automotive manufacturing, where precise torque specifications are required.

In the 1960s, the impact wrench was invented. The impact wrench is a power tool that uses compressed air to deliver high torque output. The impact wrench revolutionized the automotive industry, as it allowed mechanics to work more quickly and efficiently on assembly lines.

In recent years, wrenches have continued to evolve, and new materials and designs have been developed to make them more effective and efficient. Today, wrenches are made from a variety of materials, including steel, aluminum, and titanium. They come in a wide range of sizes and designs, from the simple adjustable wrench to the complex torque wrench.

70 LIQUID PAPER

Liquid Paper is a correction fluid used to cover up errors made while typing or writing. It was first invented by a woman named Bette Nesmith Graham in the 1950s. Liquid Paper revolutionized the way people corrected their mistakes, as it allowed them to quickly and easily cover up errors without having to start over from scratch.

Before the invention of Liquid Paper, correcting errors was a time-consuming and frustrating process. People had to use erasers, which often left smudges and marks on the page, or start over completely. Bette Nesmith Graham, who was a secretary at a bank, came up with the idea for Liquid Paper to make her own typing easier.

In the early days of Liquid Paper, Graham made the product herself at home, using a blender to mix water, white tempera paint, and other ingredients. She would then use a small brush to apply the correction fluid to her mistakes, allowing her to cover them up quickly and easily.

Graham's co-workers soon noticed how effective her invention was and began asking her to make bottles for them as well. As demand for the product grew, Graham decided to turn her invention into a business. She founded the Mistake Out Company and began selling Liquid Paper in stores across the United States.

The early versions of Liquid Paper were relatively crude compared to the modern product. The fluid was thick and difficult to spread evenly, and it often took several coats to completely cover up a mistake. Over time, Graham and her team refined the formula, making it thinner and easier to apply.

By the 1960s, Liquid Paper had become a household name, and Graham had become a millionaire thanks to her invention. She used her wealth to support various causes, including the arts and education.

In the 1970s, Liquid Paper faced a challenge from a rival product called Wite-Out, which was invented by a man named George Kloosterhouse. Wite-Out was a similar correction fluid, but it was white instead of Graham's pale blue Liquid Paper. Wite-Out quickly became popular among consumers, and its success threatened to push Liquid Paper out of the market.

In response, Graham's company began producing its own white correction fluid, called "Mistake-Out." The new product was a hit, and Liquid Paper continued to be a top-selling correction fluid throughout the 1980s and 1990s.

Over the years, Liquid Paper has gone through a few changes. The product is now available in a variety of colors and formulations, including quick-drying and odorless options. The packaging has also been updated, with the classic glass bottles giving way to plastic squeeze tubes.

In the early 2000s, the Liquid Paper brand was acquired by Newell Brands, a company that specializes in office supplies. Today, Liquid Paper is still widely used by students, office workers, and anyone who needs to correct mistakes in their writing or typing.

71 WHEELCHAIRS

The history of wheelchairs dates to ancient times when the first known evidence of wheeled furniture was found in the form of a child's bed in a cave in Orkney, Scotland, dating back to around 1300 BC. However, the use of wheeled chairs as a mobility aid for people with disabilities did not become widespread until much later.

In the 16th century, King Phillip II of Spain commissioned a rolling chair with a backrest and footrest for his royal physician, who had difficulty moving around. This was one of the earliest recorded instances of a wheelchair being used for mobility purposes.

The next major development in wheelchair technology came in the 18th century when John Dawson, an English paraplegic, invented a self-propelling wheelchair that could be operated by turning a crank. However, this wheelchair was heavy and difficult to maneuver, and it did not become widely used.

In the early 19th century, the first lightweight and more maneuverable wheelchairs were invented. These were made of wood and had two large front wheels and two small rear wheels. They were often propelled by a second person pushing from behind.

In the mid-19th century, the first folding wheelchair was invented by an American inventor named James Henry Jennings. His design used a hinged frame that could be folded up for easy storage and transportation. This was a breakthrough in wheelchair technology, as it allowed people with disabilities to be more mobile and independent.

In the late 19th and early 20th centuries, there were significant advances in wheelchair design and manufacturing. Steel replaced wood as the primary material used to construct wheelchairs, making them lighter and more durable. Pneumatic tires were also introduced, providing a smoother ride over uneven surfaces.

During World War I and World War II, wheelchairs were used extensively to transport injured soldiers. This led to further advancements in wheelchair design, including the development of electric wheelchairs in the 1950s. Electric wheelchairs were initially heavy and expensive, but improvements in technology have made them lighter and more affordable over time.

In the latter half of the 20th century, there were significant advancements in wheelchair accessibility and design. The Americans with Disabilities Act of 1990 mandated that public buildings and transportation must be accessible to people with disabilities, including those who use wheelchairs. This led to the widespread adoption of features like wheelchair ramps, wider doorways, and accessible bathrooms.

Today, wheelchairs come in a variety of designs and styles, including manual and electric models. Manual wheelchairs are operated by the user or a caregiver, while electric wheelchairs are powered by a motor. Both types of wheelchairs can be customized to fit the needs of the user, with options like adjustable seat height, backrest angle, and footrests.

Wheelchairs have come a long way since their inception, and they continue to evolve to better serve the needs of people with disabilities. Advances in technology and accessibility have made wheelchairs more comfortable, more maneuverable, and more widely available than ever before.

72 TRUMPETS

The trumpet is a brass musical instrument that has a long and storied history. Its unique sound and versatility have made it a popular instrument across cultures and throughout time. From ancient times to modern-day jazz and classical music, the trumpet has played a significant role in the development of music.

The trumpet's origins can be traced back to ancient civilizations such as Egypt and Greece, where it was used in military and religious ceremonies. The Egyptians used the trumpet as a signal for the start of battle, while the Greeks used it during religious processions and athletic competitions.

In medieval Europe, the trumpet was primarily used as a signaling instrument for military purposes. Its high pitch and clear tone made it effective for communication on the battlefield. Trumpets were also used in courts and religious ceremonies, often played in ensembles with other instruments such as horns and drums.

During the Renaissance period, the trumpet began to be used in orchestral music. Composers such as Giovanni Gabrieli and Claudio Monteverdi wrote pieces that featured the trumpet, which was now being played in a more melodic style rather than just for signaling purposes.

The Baroque period saw further developments in trumpet playing, with the introduction of valves in the late 18th century. Prior to this, trumpets were limited to playing only a few notes, and players had to rely on changing the instrument's length by adding or removing crooks. With the invention of valves, the trumpet became much more versatile and was now able to play on a full chromatic scale.

In the 19th century, the trumpet became a prominent instrument in orchestral music, and virtuosos such as Franz Xaver Richter and Louis Armstrong helped to popularize the instrument. The trumpet's sound was now being used in a wide variety of genres, from classical music to jazz and even popular music.

During the 20th century, the trumpet continued to evolve, with the introduction of new materials and manufacturing techniques. The introduction of the jazz trumpet in the early 1900s, played by musicians such as Buddy Bolden and King Oliver, brought a new style of playing to the instrument. Jazz trumpeters such as Louis Armstrong, Dizzy Gillespie, and Miles Davis helped to shape the sound of jazz music, using the trumpet to create complex and improvisational melodies.

The use of the trumpet in popular music also increased during the 20th century, with artists such as Herb Alpert and Chuck Mangione achieving chart success with their trumpet-led hits. The trumpet has also been used in rock music, with bands such as Queen and Pink Floyd featuring trumpet parts in their songs.

Today, the trumpet continues to be a popular instrument in a wide range of musical genres. Trumpeters such as Wynton Marsalis and Alison Balsom have helped to bring the trumpet to a new generation of listeners, while classical composers such as John Williams and Philip Glass continue to incorporate the instrument into their works.

In terms of design, the modern trumpet has remained largely unchanged since the introduction of valves in the 19th century. The instrument consists of a metal tube with a flared bell at one end and three valves that can be pressed down to change the pitch of the notes played. The trumpet is played by buzzing the lips into a cup-shaped mouthpiece, which produces the instrument's distinctive sound.

73 TOASTERS

The history of toasters dates to the early 1900s when electricity was first becoming a common feature in households. The first electric toaster was invented in 1905 by a man named Albert Marsh, and it was called the "Eclipse." This toaster had a wire element that heated up when electricity was applied to it, and it could toast one side of a slice of bread at a time.

The first commercially successful toaster was invented by a man named Charles Strite in 1919. Strite's toaster, called the "Toastmaster," had a timer that allowed the user to choose how long the bread would be toasted for. This toaster also had a wire element that heated up and toasted both sides of the bread at the same time. The Toastmaster became incredibly popular, and it paved the way for the modern toaster.

In the 1920s and 1930s, several other companies began to produce toasters, including General Electric, Westinghouse, and Sunbeam. These toasters were designed to be stylish as well as functional, and they often featured chrome or stainless-steel exteriors.

During World War II, toaster production slowed down as resources were diverted to the war effort. However, after the war ended, toaster production resumed, and manufacturers began to experiment with new designs and features.

In the 1950s, toasters began to feature pop-up mechanisms that would automatically eject the bread when it was done toasting. This feature made toasting bread even more convenient and popularized the use of toasters in households.

In the 1960s, toasters began to incorporate more advanced technology, including automatic shut-off switches and temperature control settings. This made toasting bread even more precise and customizable.

In the 1970s, toasters began to incorporate more advanced features such as bagel toasting capabilities and wider slots that could accommodate thicker slices of bread. These features made toasters even more versatile and useful in the kitchen.

In the 1980s and 1990s, toasters continued to evolve, and manufacturers began to experiment with different shapes and sizes. Some toasters were designed to be smaller and more portable, while others were designed to be larger and more powerful.

Today, toasters continue to be an essential kitchen appliance, and they are available in a wide range of styles, sizes, and features. Some toasters even come with digital displays and built-in sensors that can detect when the bread is done toasting.

In addition to traditional toasters, there are now also toaster ovens, which can be used for a wide range of cooking tasks in addition to toasting bread. Toaster ovens are larger than traditional toasters and can be used to bake, broil, and roast a wide range of foods.

74 PAINT ROLLERS

Paint rollers are a popular painting tool that has become a staple for both professional and DIY painters. Paint rollers are easy to use and can quickly cover large areas with a smooth finish. But where did the idea for paint rollers come from, and how have they evolved over time?

The earliest known use of a paint roller dates to 1845, when a patent was granted to Richard M. Johnson of England for a "painting machine." This machine used a revolving cylinder covered in woolen cloth to apply paint to surfaces. However, this machine was not very practical for most people due to its size and complexity.

It wasn't until 1940 that the modern paint roller was invented by Norman Breakey of Toronto, Canada. Breakey was a painter who was frustrated with the time-consuming and messy process of painting large surfaces with a brush. He began experimenting with different materials and designs until he came up with the basic design of the modern paint roller.

Breakey's paint roller consisted of a handle, a frame, and a roller cover made of mohair fabric. This design was a significant improvement over previous painting machines because it was lightweight, easy to use, and produced a smooth finish.

In the 1950s, the use of paint rollers became widespread, and the design of the roller covers began to evolve. Instead of mohair, synthetic fabrics such as nylon and polyester were introduced. These materials were more durable and easier to clean than mohair, making them ideal for use with water-based paints.

Another significant advancement in the design of paint rollers came in the 1970s when foam rollers were introduced. Foam rollers were made from a polyurethane foam that was coated with a thin layer of plastic. These rollers were ideal for use with gloss paints because they produced a smooth, even finish.

In the 1980s, textured rollers were introduced. These rollers had a patterned surface that could create a variety of textured finishes, such as stippling and ragging. Textured rollers are still widely used today and are popular with DIY painters who want to add some personality to their walls.

In recent years, advancements in technology have led to the development of even more specialized paint rollers. For example, microfiber rollers are designed to hold more paint and produce a smoother finish than traditional roller covers. Additionally, paint rollers with built-in reservoirs have been developed, allowing painters to apply paint more efficiently and without having to constantly reload the roller.

75 SCOTCH TAPE

Scotch Tape is a household name and has been for nearly a century. It's hard to imagine a world without it, as it's so prevalent in our lives. But where did this sticky invention come from? And how has it evolved over the years?

The history of Scotch Tape can be traced back to the early 20th century, when a young engineer named Richard Drew began working for the 3M company. Drew was tasked with developing a new type of masking tape that would be stronger and more reliable than anything on the market. In the course of his work, Drew stumbled upon a revolutionary idea: instead of using a weak adhesive that was easily removed, he could create a tape with a much stronger adhesive that would stick to almost anything.

Drew's idea was met with skepticism at first, but he persisted in his research and experimentation. After several years of trial and error, Drew finally developed the world's first Scotch Tape in 1930. The tape was made with a unique combination of cellulose acetate film and a strong, pressure-sensitive adhesive. The result was a tape that was incredibly strong, durable, and could be used for a wide range of applications.

The name "Scotch Tape" was originally a play on the fact that the tape was made by the Minnesota Mining and Manufacturing Company (3M), which was based in St. Paul, Minnesota. The word "Scotch" was often used as a slang term for things that were frugal or inexpensive, so the name was meant to convey the idea that the tape was affordable and reliable.

The first Scotch Tape was a hit with consumers and quickly became a household staple. It was used for everything from wrapping gifts to taping up broken windows during World War II. In fact, Scotch Tape was so popular that it became a generic term for any type of transparent adhesive tape, much like "Kleenex" is often used to refer to any brand of facial tissue.

Over the years, 3M continued to refine and improve the formula for Scotch Tape. In the 1940s, they introduced the first "magic tape," which was coated with a special adhesive that could be written on with a pen or pencil. This made it ideal for labeling and organizing, and it quickly became a favorite of office workers and homemakers alike.

In the 1950s, 3M introduced the first Scotch Tape dispenser, which made it even easier to use the tape for a variety of tasks. The dispenser allowed users to cut the tape to the exact length they needed, and it helped prevent the tape from getting tangled or stuck to itself.

In the 1960s and 1970s, 3M continued to innovate with Scotch Tape. They introduced different types of tape for different applications, such as double-sided tape for mounting photos and posters, and removable tape for temporary labeling and decorating.

Today, Scotch Tape is still one of the most popular brands of adhesive tape in the world. It's used for everything from wrapping presents to hanging up holiday decorations, and it's available in a wide range of styles and sizes to meet the needs of consumers.

In recent years, 3M has continued to innovate with Scotch Tape. They've introduced new formulas that are even stronger and more durable than before, and they've developed new types of tape that can be used in extreme conditions, such as high temperatures or wet environments.

In addition to its practical uses, Scotch Tape has also become a cultural icon. It's been featured in countless movies and TV shows, and it's even been used as a metaphor for holding things together in times of stress or crisis.

76 DUMBBELLS

The history of dumbbells dates to ancient Greece, where they were used as a form of weight training for athletes. The original design of dumbbells consisted of a single weight that was attached to a handle, which was then used to perform exercises such as curls, presses, and flies. Over the years, the design of dumbbells has evolved to include a variety of shapes and sizes, as well as different materials.

In the early days, dumbbells were made of stone or metal, and were often used in pairs. The Greeks used them for strength training, while the Romans used them for physical rehabilitation. In fact, it was the Romans who first coined the term "dumbbell," which comes from the Latin word "dumbellus," meaning "small bell."

As time went on, the use of dumbbells spread beyond ancient Greece and Rome. In the 16th century, German strongmen began using dumbbells as part of their strength training routines. These early dumbbells were made of wood and featured a cylindrical shape with a handle in the middle.

By the 17th century, dumbbells had become popular in England, where they were used in public gyms and fitness centers. The design of dumbbells continued to evolve, with some featuring ornate decorations and others featuring a more utilitarian design.

In the 18th and 19th centuries, dumbbells became a popular tool for physical culture enthusiasts, who believed in the importance of physical fitness and exercise. These enthusiasts often used dumbbells as part of their strength training routines, which also included exercises such as calisthenics, gymnastics, and weightlifting.

During the early 20th century, dumbbells became a staple of weight training and bodybuilding. This was due in part to the work of physical culture pioneers such as Eugene Sandow and Bernarr Macfadden, who popularized the idea of using weights to build muscle and improve overall fitness.

As the popularity of weight training grew, so did the variety of dumbbell designs. Dumbbells were now made of a variety of materials, including steel, cast iron, and rubber. They came in a range of shapes and sizes, from small hand-held weights to massive barbell-style dumbbells that required two hands to lift.

Today, dumbbells remain a popular tool for strength training and fitness. They are used by athletes, bodybuilders, and fitness enthusiasts of all levels. Modern dumbbells come in a variety of materials and designs, including adjustable dumbbells that allow users to change the weight of the dumbbell by adding or removing weight plates.

One of the advantages of dumbbells is their versatility. They can be used to perform a wide range of exercises, including curls, presses, flies, squats, lunges, and more. This makes them a great tool for building strength and muscle mass, as well as improving overall fitness.

Dumbbells are also relatively easy to use, making them a popular choice for home fitness enthusiasts. Unlike other weight training equipment, such as barbells and weight machines, dumbbells require minimal setup and can be easily stored when not in use.

In addition to their physical benefits, dumbbells have also been shown to have mental health benefits. Regular exercise with dumbbells can help reduce stress and anxiety, improve mood and self-esteem, and increase overall feelings of well-being.

77 TREADMILLS

The treadmill is a piece of fitness equipment that has been around for centuries. While it may be associated with modern gym culture, the treadmill has a history that dates to ancient times. From punishment to medical treatment to a workout tool, treadmills have had a variety of uses throughout history.

The earliest known version of the treadmill dates to ancient Greece in the 5th century BCE. It was called the "treadwheel," and it was used as a method of punishment for criminals. The device consisted of a large wheel with steps on the outside, and prisoners would have to climb up the steps while the wheel turned. This was a grueling and exhausting task, and it was often used as a form of hard labor.

In the 19th century, treadmills were used as a method of grinding grain and powering machinery. The treadwheel was still in use, but it was now being used to power mills and other machines. It was during this time that the first treadmills for exercise were developed.

The first patent for a treadmill designed for exercise was filed in 1843 by William Cubitt, an English engineer. Cubitt's design was meant to be used to maintain the fitness of factory workers. The machine was powered by a person walking on a belt that moved over a series of rollers.

In the late 1800s, Dr. Gustav Zander, a Swedish physician, developed a series of exercise machines, including a treadmill. Zander's machines were designed to improve the health and fitness of his patients, and they were used in hospitals and clinics throughout Europe. Zander's treadmills were powered by the user's own energy, and they were designed to mimic the movements of walking and running.

The first electric treadmill was developed in 1952 by Dr. Robert Bruce, a cardiologist. Bruce was looking for a way to test the endurance of his patients, and he designed a treadmill that could be used for this purpose. The machine was motorized, and it had adjustable speeds and inclines.

In the 1960s, treadmills began to gain popularity as a form of exercise equipment. They were initially used by athletes and runners to train indoors, but they soon became a popular tool for general fitness and weight loss.

In the 1970s, the first home treadmills were developed, making it easier for people to exercise at home. These early home treadmills were often bulky and expensive, but they paved the way for the more advanced and affordable models that are available today.

Since the 1980s, treadmills have become a staple of gyms and fitness centers around the world. They are now available in a variety of sizes and designs, from small folding models for home use to commercial-grade machines for use in fitness facilities.

Today, treadmills are used for a variety of purposes, from general fitness and weight loss to rehabilitation and sports training. They are often used in combination with other types of exercise equipment, such as weights and resistance bands, to create a comprehensive workout routine.

In recent years, there has been a trend toward using treadmills for more than just running and walking. Many modern treadmills come with built-in programs and features, such as incline training and virtual reality simulations, that make the workout experience more engaging and varied.

78 TRAMPOLINES

The trampoline is a popular recreational device that is enjoyed by people of all ages. It is a flexible piece of equipment that consists of a sheet of fabric stretched over a metal frame, which is then attached to a series of springs that allow it to bounce users up and down. The history of the trampoline is an interesting one, beginning with its invention in the early 20th century.

The trampoline was first invented in 1934 by George Nissen and Larry Griswold, two gymnasts from the University of Iowa. They had been experimenting with various methods of improving their tumbling skills when they hit upon the idea of stretching a piece of canvas over a metal frame and using it to bounce themselves higher and higher.

Initially, they called their invention a "bouncing rig," but later settled on the name "trampoline," which was derived from the Spanish word "trampolin," meaning "diving board." They began performing public demonstrations of their invention, and soon the trampoline became a popular attraction at circuses, fairs, and other public events.

During World War II, the trampoline found a new use as a training tool for pilots and navigators. The United States Navy began using trampolines to teach pilots how to bail out of planes and land safely in water. This was because the trampoline's bounce provided a realistic simulation of the experience of jumping from a plane and landing in water. The Navy found that pilots who had trained on the trampoline were much better equipped to handle emergency situations.

After the war, the trampoline became a popular recreational device once again. In the 1950s and 1960s, trampoline parks began popping up all over the United States, offering people a new and exciting way to have fun and get exercise. The first trampoline park, called "The Jump Spot," was opened in 1959 in Texas by the creator of the first modern trampoline, George Nissen.

As trampolines became more popular, their design and construction began to evolve. In the early days, trampolines were made with metal frames and canvas sheets. Later, manufacturers began using synthetic materials like nylon and polyester to make the jumping surface more durable and longer lasting.

In the 1970s and 1980s, the trampoline began to be used as a competitive sport. Trampolining competitions were held all over the world, and in 2000, trampolining was recognized as an official Olympic sport. Today, trampolines are still used for recreation, but they are also an important tool for athletes and gymnasts who use them to train for various sports and competitions.

Trampolines have also found new uses in recent years. For example, rebounding, which is a type of low-impact exercise that involves bouncing on a mini trampoline, has become a popular fitness trend. Many people enjoy rebounding because it is a fun and easy way to get a great workout without putting too much strain on their joints.

In addition, trampolines are also being used in therapy and rehabilitation settings. Physical therapists and occupational therapists use trampolines to help patients regain strength, balance, and coordination after an injury or illness.

In recent years, safety concerns have also become an important issue for trampoline manufacturers and users. While trampolines are generally safe when used properly, they can be dangerous if proper safety precautions are not taken. Many trampolines now come equipped with safety features like safety nets and padding to help prevent injuries.

79 THE TELESCOPE

The telescope is an instrument that has played a significant role in the advancement of astronomy and our understanding of the universe. Its history dates to the early 17th century, when the Dutch eyeglass maker, Hans Lippershey, invented the first refracting telescope. Over time, the design of the telescope has evolved, leading to a better understanding of the universe and its workings.

The earliest telescopes were simple devices that used lenses to magnify objects. In 1608, Lippershey applied for a patent on a device that he called a "looking glass" which used two lenses to magnify objects. Shortly thereafter, another Dutchman named Jacob Metius, and an Italian scientist named Galileo Galilei, independently developed their own versions of the telescope. Galileo's telescope, which he used to observe the moons of Jupiter, was able to magnify objects up to 30 times their original size.

In the early years of the telescope, refracting telescopes were the norm. These telescopes used lenses to bend light and create an image of a distant object. However, the lenses used in these telescopes had certain limitations. For one, they were often of poor quality, resulting in blurred images. Additionally, lenses are prone to chromatic aberration, a distortion of the image caused by the different colors of light being refracted at slightly different angles.

In the 1660s, a Frenchman named Laurent Cassegrain invented the first reflecting telescope. Reflecting telescopes use mirrors instead of lenses to focus light and create an image. This eliminated many of the problems associated with refracting telescopes, including chromatic aberration. Reflecting telescopes also had the potential to be much larger than refracting telescopes, making them more powerful.

The 18th and 19th centuries saw a great deal of innovation in telescope design. One of the most significant advances came in 1789, when William Herschel built a telescope with a mirror that was 1.2 meters in diameter. This was the largest telescope in the world at the time, and it allowed Herschel to discover many new celestial objects, including the planet Uranus.

In the 19th century, telescope design continued to evolve, with the introduction of new materials and new technologies. One of the most important innovations was the development of the mountaintop observatory. These observatories were located at high altitudes, where the air was thinner, and the skies were clearer. This allowed astronomers to make more precise observations and gather more accurate data.

In the 20th century, telescope design continued to improve, with the introduction of new materials and new technologies. One of the most significant advances came in the 1930s, when the German optician Bernhard Schmidt invented the Schmidt telescope. This telescope used a specially designed curved mirror to eliminate many of the problems associated with earlier telescope designs.

The late 20th century and early 21st century saw a few important developments in telescope technology. One of the most significant was the introduction of the space telescope. In 1990, the Hubble Space Telescope was launched into orbit around the Earth. This telescope was able to gather data from space without the interference of Earth's atmosphere, allowing for even clearer and more precise observations.

Today, there are many different types of telescopes in use. Some of the most common designs include the refracting telescope, the reflecting telescope, the Cassegrain telescope, and the Schmidt telescope. Telescopes are used for a wide range of purposes, including observing celestial objects, studying the properties of light, and conducting research in fields like astrophysics and cosmology.

80 LOLLIPOPS

Lollipops are a sweet confectionary treat that has been enjoyed by people all over the world for many decades. These small, candy treats are known for their unique shape and variety of flavors. While it is not known exactly where or when lollipops were first created, there are some theories about their origin and development over the years.

One of the earliest references to a lollipop-like candy can be found in Ancient Egypt. Archaeologists have uncovered evidence of a candy made from honey and fruit that was shaped like a stick, which may have been used as a type of medicine to soothe sore throats or coughs. Similar candies were also found in Ancient Greece and Rome, where they were called "rhombus" and "spira," respectively.

However, it wasn't until the 17th century that lollipops as we know them today began to take shape. In England, sugar was becoming more widely available and affordable, and people began to experiment with different ways of using it. One popular treat was a hard candy that was formed into a ball and attached to a stick, which was called a "sucker."

These early lollipops were typically made by boiling sugar and water together until it reached a high temperature, then pouring the mixture into molds to harden. The sticks were then inserted into the center of the candy, creating a handle that made it easier to eat.

Lollipops became increasingly popular throughout the 19th century, as new techniques for mass-producing candy made them more affordable and accessible to a wider range of people. In the United States, the first machine for making lollipops was invented in 1908 by George Smith, who founded the American Lollipop Company.

By the 1920s, lollipops had become a staple of American candy culture, with dozens of different brands and flavors available. Many of these early lollipops were marketed towards children, with colorful packaging and fun shapes that made them an appealing treat for kids of all ages.

During World War II, lollipops became a popular treat for soldiers, who often carried them in their pockets as a quick source of energy and a reminder of home. In the years following the war, lollipops continued to evolve, with new flavors and shapes being introduced to keep up with changing consumer tastes.

In the 1960s, the first "gourmet" lollipops began to appear, made with high-quality ingredients and featuring unique flavors like champagne and coffee. These high-end lollipops were often sold in specialty shops and marketed towards adults, reflecting the growing interest in gourmet food and artisanal products during the era.

Today, lollipops remain a popular treat around the world, with a wide range of flavors and varieties available to suit every taste. While they may have started out as a simple candy on a stick, lollipops have evolved into a diverse and beloved part of candy culture, with a rich history and ongoing legacy of innovation and creativity.

81 COMPACT DISCS

The history of Compact Discs, or CDs, is one of innovation and transformation in the world of music and technology. CDs were introduced in the early 1980s and rapidly became the standard format for music storage, replacing vinyl records and cassette tapes. The development of CDs was a major turning point in the music industry and marked the beginning of the digital age of music.

The origins of the CD can be traced back to the early 1970s when a joint venture was formed between Sony and Philips, two of the world's leading electronics companies. The aim of this collaboration was to create a new type of audio recording medium that would be more durable and higher quality than existing formats such as vinyl records and cassette tapes.

After years of research and development, the first CD was unveiled in 1982. The disc was a 12cm plastic disc coated with a thin layer of aluminum and covered with a layer of plastic. The disc had a capacity of 74 minutes and could hold up to 650MB of digital data. CDs were read using a laser beam, which scanned the disc and translated the data into sound.

The introduction of CDs was a major event in the music industry. For the first time, music could be recorded and played back without the hiss and crackle associated with vinyl records or the occasional dropouts that occurred with cassette tapes. CDs were also far more durable than other formats, and the sound quality was consistently high regardless of how many times the disc was played.

CDs rapidly became the standard format for music storage, and the music industry was quick to capitalize on the new technology. Record companies began to reissue their back catalogs on CD, and new releases were almost always released on the format. The rise of the CD also coincided with the explosion of the CD player market. As the price of CD players came down, more and more consumers bought into the format, and the CD became the dominant music medium of the 1980s and 1990s.

However, the rise of the CD was not without its problems. The move to digital technology was controversial in some circles, and there were concerns that CDs would lead to a decline in sound quality. Some audiophiles argued that CDs lacked the warmth and depth of vinyl records, and that the compressed sound of the CD was a poor substitute for the live performance. There were also concerns that CDs were prone to skipping, particularly in cars or other moving environments.

Despite these concerns, the CD remained the dominant music medium for almost two decades. However, the advent of the internet and the rise of digital music changed the landscape of the music industry once again. The introduction of MP3s and digital music players such as the iPod allowed consumers to carry their entire music collections in their pockets, and the demand for CDs began to decline rapidly.

In recent years, CDs have been largely superseded by digital music downloads and streaming services such as Spotify and Apple Music. However, the legacy of the CD lives on, and many music fans still value the physicality and tangible nature of the format. Today, CDs are often purchased by collectors and audiophiles, and some music lovers argue that the sound quality of a CD is still superior to that of a digital download.

82 THE TAPE MEASURE

The tape measure is a tool that has been used for centuries to measure distance, length, and other physical dimensions. The history of the tape measure can be traced back to ancient times, when people used various measuring devices, including ropes, strings, and sticks, to measure distance.

One of the earliest known measuring devices was the cubit, which was used by the ancient Egyptians and other cultures. A cubit was a unit of measure that was based on the length of a person's forearm from the elbow to the tip of the middle finger. Over time, other measuring devices were developed, including the rod, which was a long stick or pole that was used to measure distances.

During the medieval period, various types of measuring devices were used by craftsmen and builders. These included measuring sticks, yardsticks, and rods, which were made from wood or metal. The sticks were marked with measurements that allowed craftsmen to accurately measure the length and width of their workpieces.

In the 16th century, tape measures began to appear. These early tape measures were made from materials such as linen, silk, or cotton, and were marked with measurements in inches or feet. They were typically used by tailors and seamstresses to measure fabric.

The first patent for a tape measure was issued in the United States in 1868 to Alvin J. Fellows. Fellows' tape measure was made from a strip of spring steel that was coiled up into a small metal case. The tape could be pulled out of the case and locked in place using a button on the side. This design made it easy to use the tape measure with one hand.

In the 20th century, tape measures became more sophisticated and were made from a variety of materials, including plastics and metals. The accuracy of tape measures was improved using laser technology, which allowed for measurements to be taken with greater precision.

Today, tape measures are widely used in a variety of industries, including construction, woodworking, and manufacturing. They come in a range of lengths and styles, from small pocket-sized tape measures to large industrial models that can measure distances of up to 100 feet or more.

One of the most popular types of tape measures is the retractable tape measure. This type of tape measure has a spring-loaded mechanism that allows the tape to be retracted into a small case when not in use. Retractable tape measures are compact and easy to carry, making them ideal for use on job sites and in workshops.

Another popular type of tape measure is the digital tape measure. Digital tape measures use electronic sensors to measure distance and display the measurement on a digital readout. These types of tape measures are often used in industries where high levels of accuracy are required, such as in engineering and manufacturing.

In recent years, there has been a growing trend towards using smartphone apps and other digital tools for measuring distances and dimensions. However, tape measures remain an essential tool for many professionals and hobbyists who require accurate and reliable measurements.

.

83 CURTAINS

Curtains have been used for thousands of years to provide privacy, regulate light, and add a decorative touch to homes and other spaces. The history of curtains can be traced back to ancient civilizations such as Egypt, Greece, and Rome, where they were primarily used for practical purposes.

In ancient Egypt, curtains were made of fine linen and used to divide rooms and protect the privacy of occupants. They were also used to create a sense of grandeur in temples and other public buildings. Greek and Roman civilizations also used curtains for similar purposes, but they were often made of heavier materials such as wool and hung on wooden rods.

During the Middle Ages, curtains were primarily used in churches and castles to provide insulation and privacy. They were often made of heavy tapestries and hung on large iron rings or hooks. It wasn't until the Renaissance period that curtains began to be used more widely in homes.

In the 16th and 17th centuries, curtains became a symbol of wealth and status. They were often made of rich fabrics such as silk, velvet, and brocade and adorned with intricate embroidery or lace. The use of curtains in this way continued throughout the 18th and 19th centuries, particularly in grand homes and palaces.

The Industrial Revolution brought about significant changes in the way curtains were made. The development of power looms and other machinery made it possible to produce curtains on a larger scale and at a lower cost. This made curtains more accessible to the middle and lower classes.

The Victorian era saw a resurgence in the use of heavy curtains with elaborate trimmings and fringes. They were often used in combination with drapes and swags to create a grandiose look. However, the invention of lighter weight materials such as muslin and voile in the late 19th century led to a shift towards lighter, more airy curtains.

The 20th century saw a further evolution of curtains with the introduction of new materials such as polyester and nylon. These materials were durable, easy to clean, and more affordable than traditional fabrics. They also allowed for a wider range of colors and patterns.

During the mid-20th century, curtains became a popular means of expressing personal style and creativity. The use of bold prints and patterns in bright colors became fashionable, and many people began making their own curtains at home.

In recent years, curtains have continued to evolve with the introduction of new materials and technology. Smart curtains that can be controlled by smartphones or other devices have become increasingly popular, and energy-efficient curtains that help regulate temperature and save energy have also become more common.

Today, curtains are available in a wide range of styles, materials, and colors to suit any taste and budget. From simple, minimalist designs to elaborate, ornate styles, there is a curtain to fit every need and preference.

The Stupid History Book

84 SLIPPERS

Slippers are a type of footwear that have been worn for centuries. They are a simple, comfortable shoe that is easy to slip on and off, and they have been worn by people all over the world for a variety of reasons.

The history of slippers can be traced back to ancient times, when people wore simple shoes made from animal hides and fur. These early slippers were likely worn by people in cold climates who needed to keep their feet warm and protected from the elements. In some cultures, slippers were also worn indoors as a sign of respect, to keep floors clean, or as part of religious or cultural ceremonies.

In ancient Egypt, for example, slippers were worn by both men and women as a symbol of their social status. The pharaohs and other high-ranking officials wore elaborate slippers made from precious materials like gold and silver, while commoners wore simpler slippers made from woven reeds or papyrus. In Japan, traditional slippers called zori have been worn for centuries as part of the country's cultural heritage. These slippers are made from straw or other natural materials and are worn indoors as a sign of respect.

In medieval Europe, slippers were often worn by wealthy nobles as a sign of their status. These slippers were made from expensive materials like velvet, silk, and fur, and were often adorned with jewels or embroidery. They were worn indoors to keep floors clean and to show off one's wealth and status.

In the 18th and 19th centuries, slippers became more popular as a type of leisure footwear. Wealthy women would wear delicate slippers made from silk or satin, often adorned with lace or embroidery, to relax and feel

169

comfortable at home. Men's slippers were also popular during this time and were often made from leather or velvet.

In the 20th century, slippers became more practical and comfortable, with many people wearing them for both indoor and outdoor activities. During World War II, soldiers were issued slippers as part of their standard gear, as they were easy to wear and provided some protection for their feet. In the 1950s and 60s, slippers became popular as a type of casual footwear, with many people wearing them as a comfortable alternative to shoes or sandals.

Today, slippers are still a popular type of footwear, worn by people of all ages and backgrounds. They come in a wide range of styles and materials, from simple cotton slippers to luxurious leather or shearling slippers. Some slippers are designed for specific activities, like yoga or indoor sports, while others are made for general wear around the house or as a comfortable option for travel.

In recent years, slippers have also become a popular fashion accessory, with many designers creating stylish and trendy slippers for both men and women. Celebrities like Rihanna and Justin Bieber have even launched their own lines of slippers, further cementing their place in modern fashion culture.

85 CHOCOLATE CHIPS

The history of chocolate chips is a story that is intertwined with the development of the chocolate industry in the United States. The invention of chocolate chips can be traced back to the early 1930s and has since become a staple ingredient in a variety of baked goods, such as chocolate chip cookies.

The story of chocolate chips begins with Ruth Wakefield, who owned the Toll House Inn in Whitman, Massachusetts. In 1930, Wakefield was making a batch of cookies for her guests when she realized she was out of baker's chocolate. Instead of using another type of chocolate, she decided to break up a bar of Nestle's semi-sweet chocolate into small pieces and add them to the cookie dough.

To her surprise, the chocolate pieces did not melt completely and instead stayed in chunks throughout the cookie. This happy accident led to the creation of the first chocolate chip cookie, which quickly became popular with Wakefield's guests.

Wakefield's creation did not go unnoticed by Nestle, which saw an opportunity to market its chocolate to home bakers. In 1939, the company introduced its own pre-cut chocolate chunks under the brand name "Nestle Toll House Chocolate Morsels," which became the first commercially available chocolate chips.

The popularity of chocolate chips grew quickly, especially during World War II when soldiers were given chocolate chip cookies as part of their rations. The cookies became a symbol of home and comfort for the soldiers, and when they returned home, they continued to enjoy them with their families.

As the popularity of chocolate chips grew, other companies began to produce their own versions. In the 1950s, Hershey's introduced its own brand of chocolate chips, followed by Ghirardelli and others.

In the 1970s, the introduction of the chocolate chip cookie dough in a tube revolutionized the way people made cookies at home. Pillsbury's "Slice 'n Bake" cookies made it easy for anyone to bake a fresh batch of chocolate chip cookies without the hassle of measuring and mixing ingredients.

The popularity of chocolate chips also led to the creation of other chocolate chip products, such as chocolate chip ice cream and chocolate chip granola bars. Today, chocolate chips are used in a variety of baked goods, from cookies and brownies to cakes and muffins.

In recent years, there has been a growing demand for high-quality chocolate chips made with premium ingredients. Artisanal chocolate makers have begun producing their own chocolate chips, using single-origin chocolate and natural ingredients. These premium chocolate chips have a richer, more complex flavor than their mass-produced counterparts and are often used in gourmet desserts and baked goods.

86 THE MAGNIFYING GLASS

The magnifying glass is a simple yet incredibly useful optical instrument that has been used for centuries to magnify and inspect small objects. Its history dates to ancient times, and its evolution has been intertwined with the development of optics and lenses.

The earliest known reference to the use of a magnifying glass dates to ancient Egypt, where it is believed that a convex lens made of quartz was used to magnify objects. However, it was not until the 13th century that the first practical magnifying glass was invented in Europe.

The inventor of the first practical magnifying glass is not known, but it is believed to have been a craftsman or artisan who discovered that by grinding a piece of glass into a convex shape, it could magnify objects when held close to the eye. These early magnifying glasses were small and handheld, with the glass mounted in a metal or wooden frame.

By the 14th century, the use of magnifying glasses had become more widespread, and they were being used in various fields such as art, science, and medicine. The Italian painter and architect Filippo Brunelleschi used a magnifying glass to study and copy ancient Roman sculptures, while the German scientist Johannes Kepler used a magnifying glass to study the moon and stars.

In the 17th century, the Dutch scientist Antonie van Leeuwenhoek revolutionized the use of the magnifying glass by developing a powerful microscope. Leeuwenhoek's microscope was made of a tiny glass bead that was mounted in a metal holder and could magnify objects up to 200 times their original size. With this new tool, Leeuwenhoek was able to observe and document microorganisms, which he called "animalcules," for the first time.

The 18th century saw further advancements in the field of optics, with the development of achromatic lenses, which corrected for the distortion caused by the different colors of light. These lenses made it possible to create more precise and powerful magnifying glasses, which were used in a wide range of applications, from astronomy to surgery.

In the 19th century, the invention of the compound microscope, which used a series of lenses to magnify objects, replaced the simple magnifying glass in many scientific applications. However, the magnifying glass continued to be widely used in everyday life, from reading glasses to handheld magnifiers used by jewelers and stamp collectors.

In the 20th century, the magnifying glass continued to evolve with the development of new materials and manufacturing techniques. Today, magnifying glasses are made of a variety of materials, including plastic, glass, and acrylic, and come in a range of sizes and magnification strengths.

In addition to traditional handheld magnifying glasses, there are now also magnifying glasses that can be attached to smartphones and tablets, allowing users to magnify text and images on their screens. These devices have been particularly helpful for people with visual impairments, allowing them to read and access information more easily.

87 THE DVD

The DVD, or Digital Versatile Disc, is a digital optical disc format used for storing and playing high-quality audio and video content. It was developed in the 1990s as a successor to the CD, and quickly became the dominant format for home video entertainment.

The history of the DVD can be traced back to the early 1990s, when a group of companies including Philips, Sony, and Toshiba began working on a new type of disc format that could hold more data than a CD. The result was the creation of the DVD, which was officially launched in 1995.

The first DVD players were released in Japan in November 1996, and soon after in the United States and Europe. These early DVD players were expensive and only supported a limited number of features, but they quickly gained popularity due to their superior image and sound quality compared to VHS tapes.

One of the key factors that helped the DVD gain widespread acceptance was the release of major Hollywood movies on the format. In 1997, Warner Bros. became the first studio to release a film on DVD with the release of "Twister". Other studios quickly followed suit, and by 2000, over 2,700 movies were available on DVD.

In addition to movies, the DVD format also became popular for storing and distributing music albums. The improved sound quality and ability to include additional content like music videos and behind-the-scenes footage made it an attractive alternative to CDs.

The DVD format continued to evolve throughout the late 1990s and early

2000s, with the introduction of new features like DVD-ROMs (which could be used to store data like computer software), dual-layer discs (which could hold twice as much data as a single-layer disc), and the introduction of the DVD+R and DVD-R formats (which allowed consumers to record their own content onto DVDs).

Despite the introduction of new formats like Blu-ray and streaming services like Netflix, the DVD remained the dominant format for home video entertainment well into the 2000s. In 2003, DVD sales surpassed VHS sales for the first time, and by 2006, DVDs accounted for over 90% of all home video sales.

However, as technology continued to evolve, the popularity of DVDs began to decline. The rise of streaming services like Netflix and the increased availability of digital downloads meant that consumers had more options for accessing movies and TV shows than ever before.

By the early 2010s, DVD sales had fallen significantly, and many retailers began to reduce the amount of floor space devoted to DVDs in their stores. In 2013, Best Buy announced that it would no longer sell CDs or DVDs in its stores, and many other retailers followed suit.

Despite the decline of the format, DVDs continue to be used in certain industries, such as education and healthcare, where they are used for training and informational purposes. And while the format may no longer be as popular as it once was, the impact of the DVD on the home entertainment industry cannot be overstated. It revolutionized the way we consume movies and TV shows, and paved the way for the digital streaming revolution that is still ongoing today.

88 ROLLER SKATES

Roller skating is a recreational activity that has been enjoyed by people for centuries. It involves wearing shoes with small wheels on the bottom and gliding or moving around on a flat surface. The concept of roller skate's dates to the 18th century, but the modern roller skates we know today were developed in the 19th century.

The first recorded instance of roller skates was in 1743 when a Belgian inventor named John Joseph Merlin created a pair of skates with small metal wheels. However, the skates were difficult to control, and the inventor himself ended up injuring himself in a public demonstration when he crashed into a mirror. Despite this initial setback, the idea of roller skates persisted, and various inventors throughout Europe and America continued to experiment with different designs.

In the 1860s, a Frenchman named Jean-Joseph Merlin improved upon the initial design by adding rubber wheels and a brake. However, the skates were still difficult to control and were mostly used for novelty acts in circus shows.

It wasn't until 1863 when an American inventor named James Leonard Plimpton created the first quad roller skate that roller skating began to gain popularity. Plimpton's design featured four wheels in a square formation, which allowed for better stability and control. He also added a pivot point that made it easier for skaters to turn and maneuver.

Plimpton's invention was an immediate success, and roller skating became a popular pastime in America and Europe. Skating rinks began to pop up in cities across the United States, and roller skating became a popular social activity for people of all ages.

In the late 19th and early 20th century, roller skating reached its peak popularity. Skating rinks were common in cities and towns across the country, and roller skating became a popular activity for families and couples. Skating clubs and competitions were also established, and roller skating became a competitive sport.

During this time, new innovations in roller skate design were also introduced. In 1902, an inventor named Joseph Henry Hughes created a roller skate that had adjustable trucks, which allowed skaters to adjust the tightness of the wheels for better control. In the 1930s, roller skates with ball bearings were introduced, which allowed for smoother and faster skating.

However, roller skating's popularity began to decline in the mid-20th century. The invention of the automobile made it easier for people to travel to other forms of entertainment, and roller-skating rinks began to close. Roller derby, a competitive contact sport played on roller skates, became popular in the 1950s and 1960s but also saw a decline in popularity in the 1970s.

In the 1980s and 1990s, roller skating experienced a resurgence in popularity. Roller disco, a style of skating that incorporates dance and music, became popular, and roller-skating rinks began to open again across the United States. Inline skates, which feature a line of wheels in a row, also became popular during this time.

Today, roller skating remains a popular recreational activity for people of all ages. Roller skating rinks can be found in many cities, and roller derby continues to be played as a competitive sport. Inline skating has also remained popular, and rollerblading has become a common form of transportation in many urban areas.

89 SUSPENDERS

Suspenders, also known as braces in the United Kingdom, are a type of garment accessory designed to hold up pants or trousers. They consist of straps that go over the shoulders and attach to the waistband of the pants, providing support and preventing them from falling. Suspenders have a long history that spans several centuries and continents, from their origins in the 18th century to their modern-day popularity in fashion.

The history of suspenders can be traced back to the 18th century, when men wore breeches or tight-fitting trousers that were held up by buttons or laces. However, these methods were not always effective, as pants tended to sag or slip down, especially during physical activity. In response to this problem, men began to wear suspenders, which provided a more secure and comfortable way of holding up their pants.

The earliest suspenders were simple pieces of ribbon or cloth that were tied around the waist and shoulders. However, these primitive designs were not very effective, as they tended to slip or come undone. In the late 18th century, a new type of suspender was invented that featured metal clasps or clips that could be attached to the waistband of pants. This design proved to be much more effective, and soon became popular among men of all social classes.

During the 19th century, suspenders continued to evolve and improve. In the United States, the first patented suspenders were invented by Albert Thurston in 1820. These suspenders featured leather loops that could be attached to buttons on the waistband of pants, providing a more secure and durable method of holding them up. Thurston's design became popular among men in Europe and America, and his company still produces high-quality suspenders today.

In the early 20th century, suspenders began to fall out of favor as men began to wear belts instead. Belts were cheaper and easier to produce, and they offered a more streamlined look that was favored by the fashion industry. However, suspenders continued to be worn by some men, particularly those in the working class, who found them to be more comfortable and practical for their jobs.

During the 1920s and 1930s, suspenders experienced a resurgence in popularity, thanks in part to Hollywood movie stars who wore them on screen. Actors like Fred Astaire, Cary Grant, and Clark Gable helped to make suspenders fashionable once again, and they became a popular accessory among stylish men of all ages. During this time, suspenders were often worn with high-waisted trousers, creating a classic and sophisticated look that remains popular to this day.

In the decades that followed, suspenders continued to be worn by men of all ages and social classes, although they were gradually replaced by belts as the primary method of holding up pants. However, suspenders remained a popular accessory among certain subcultures, including punks and skinheads, who wore them as a symbol of rebellion and nonconformity.

In recent years, suspenders have experienced a renewed popularity, thanks in part to the rise of vintage and retro fashion. Many men now wear suspenders as a stylish alternative to belts, and they are often paired with high-waisted pants, bow ties, and other classic accessories. Suspenders are also popular among women, who wear them as a chic and fashionable accessory with dresses, skirts, and high-waisted pants.

Today, suspenders are available in a wide variety of styles, colors, and materials, from traditional leather and silk designs to modern fabrics like nylon and elastic. They are often worn for both fashion and function, providing a comfortable and secure way of holding up pants while also adding a touch of style to any outfit.

90 LIP GLOSS

Lip gloss has been a popular cosmetic item for decades, offering a subtle shine and a pop of color to the lips. The history of lip gloss dates to the early 1900s, when cosmetics first became widely available.

One of the earliest forms of lip gloss was petroleum jelly, which was first discovered in the mid-19th century. Women would apply petroleum jelly to their lips to moisturize them and create a subtle shine. However, this early form of lip gloss was not very long-lasting and often had a greasy texture.

In the 1930s, Max Factor, a Hollywood makeup artist, created the first true lip gloss. He mixed a combination of waxes, oils, and pigments to create a product that offered a longer-lasting shine and a more vibrant color. Factor's lip gloss quickly became popular among Hollywood stars and was soon being sold to the general public.

In the 1950s, a company called Tangee began manufacturing a unique lip gloss that changed color depending on the wearer's skin tone. The product was a huge success and spawned several imitators. Other companies began experimenting with new formulas and packaging, creating lip glosses that were easier to apply and came in a wider range of colors.

By the 1960s, lip gloss had become a staple in many women's cosmetic bags. The popularity of lip gloss continued to grow throughout the 1970s and 1980s, with new brands and formulas being introduced on a regular basis. One of the most popular lip glosses of the 1980s was Bonne Bell's Lip Smacker, which came in a range of fun flavors and was marketed primarily to young girls.

In the 1990s, lip gloss took on a more high-fashion look, with many brands offering a more sophisticated range of colors and finishes. One of the most notable new products of the decade was MAC's Lipglass, which offered a highly pigmented, glossy finish that was popular with both makeup artists and consumers.

In the 2000s, lip gloss continued to be popular, with many brands introducing new formulas and packaging. One of the most innovative new products was Lancome's Juicy Tubes, which came in a tube with a sponge-tip applicator and offered a high-shine, non-sticky finish.

Today, lip gloss remains a popular cosmetic item, with a wide range of brands and formulas available. Many brands now offer lip glosses with added skincare benefits, such as moisturizing ingredients and SPF protection. There are also a few vegan and cruelty-free options available for those who prefer to shop for ethical beauty products.

While lip gloss has come a long way since its early days as a simple petroleum jelly, its popularity shows no signs of slowing down. Whether you prefer a subtle shine or a bold pop of color, there's lip gloss out there for everyone.

91 VANILLA PUDDING

Vanilla pudding is a creamy dessert that has been enjoyed for centuries. Its origins can be traced back to ancient civilizations, where it was made using various ingredients such as milk, honey, and eggs. Over time, the recipe evolved and became more refined, with the addition of new ingredients and techniques.

The history of vanilla pudding can be traced back to the early days of civilization. In ancient Greece and Rome, people would make a dish called "kustos," which was a type of pudding made with milk, honey, and eggs. This dish was often served as a dessert or as breakfast food.

During the Middle Ages, custard became a popular dessert among the upper class. It was made with cream, eggs, sugar, and spices, and was often served with fruit or nuts. As the recipe evolved, some cooks began to add starch to thicken the custard, which would later become a key ingredient in vanilla pudding.

By the 18th century, pudding had become a staple of British cuisine. Recipes for pudding varied greatly, and many were made with suet, a type of fat from beef or mutton. However, some cooks began to experiment with new ingredients, such as cornstarch and gelatin, to thicken their puddings.

It wasn't until the 19th century that vanilla pudding as we know it today began to emerge. In 1837, Alfred Bird, a chemist from England, invented a type of custard powder that could be used to make custard without eggs. This powder was a mixture of cornstarch, sugar, and flavorings, and could be easily mixed with milk to create a creamy dessert.

Bird's custard powder was an instant success, and soon became a staple in households across England. The powder was used not only to make custard, but also to create a variety of other desserts, including vanilla pudding.

In the United States, vanilla pudding became popular in the early 20th century. Recipes for pudding began to appear in cookbooks and magazines, and it quickly became a favorite dessert among Americans.

In the 1920s, Jell-O introduced a new product called "Jell-O Pudding," which was a pre-made, instant pudding mix that could be easily prepared at home. This product was a huge success and helped to popularize pudding even further.

Over the years, the recipe for vanilla pudding has continued to evolve. Today, there are many different variations of the dessert, including vegan and gluten-free options. Some recipes call for the use of whole eggs, while others use only egg yolks or cornstarch to thicken the pudding.

Despite its long and varied history, vanilla pudding remains a beloved dessert around the world. Whether served on its own or used as a filling for pies and cakes, it continues to be a popular choice for those with a sweet tooth.

92 SALTWATER TAFFY

Saltwater taffy is a delicious candy that has been enjoyed by people for generations. It is a type of chewy candy that is usually made with sugar, corn syrup, and butter. The candy is then flavored with a variety of different ingredients such as vanilla, chocolate, fruit flavors, and of course, salt.

The exact history of saltwater taffy is a bit murky, but there are a few stories that have been passed down through the generations. One of the most popular stories is that saltwater taffy was first created in the late 1800s in Atlantic City, New Jersey.

According to the story, a candy shop owner named David Bradley was working in his shop one day when a powerful storm caused seawater to flood the store. The candy that was sitting on the shelves was soaked in seawater, ruining it. However, Bradley decided to try and salvage the candy by drying it out and selling it anyway.

To his surprise, customers loved the salty taste of the candy, and they started calling it "saltwater taffy." Bradley began making the candy on purpose and selling it in his shop, and it quickly became a popular treat among visitors to Atlantic City.

Another story about the origin of saltwater taffy comes from a candy maker in the southern United States. According to this story, a candy maker was trying to create a new type of candy when he accidentally added salt instead of sugar to the recipe. He decided to see what would happen if he continued making the candy, and the result was a chewy, salty candy that he dubbed "saltwater taffy."

Regardless of which story is true, there is no denying that saltwater taffy became very popular in the late 1800s and early 1900s. The candy was sold in many different flavors and colors, and it was often packaged in decorative boxes and sold as souvenirs in seaside towns and tourist destinations.

In fact, saltwater taffy was so popular that it became a symbol of the seaside vacation experience. Many people who visited Atlantic City or other seaside towns would bring home boxes of saltwater taffy as souvenirs or gifts for friends and family.

During the early 1900s, saltwater taffy became a big business, and many candy makers began producing their own versions of the candy. In Atlantic City, several candy makers banded together to create the "Original Atlantic City Saltwater Taffy" association, which set standards for the candy's quality and helped promote it to visitors.

Today, saltwater taffy is still a popular candy that is enjoyed by people all over the world. Many seaside towns still sell saltwater taffy as a souvenir or to promote their town, and many candy makers still produce their own versions of the candy.

One of the most famous saltwater taffy makers is Fralinger's, which was founded in 1885 in Atlantic City. Fralinger's is known for its wide variety of flavors, including some unique ones like molasses mint and peanut butter.

Another famous saltwater taffy maker is James Candy Company, which was founded in 1880 in Atlantic City. James Candy Company is known for its high-quality taffy, which is made with natural flavors and colors.

93 BASEBALL CAPS

Baseball caps are a popular piece of headwear that is worn by people of all ages, genders, and backgrounds. They are often used as a fashion statement or to show support for a particular sports team, but the origins of baseball caps lie in the sport for which they are named.

The history of baseball caps can be traced back to the mid-19th century when baseball was becoming an increasingly popular sport in the United States. At that time, players wore straw hats or top hats to protect themselves from the sun during games. However, these hats were not practical for playing baseball, as they would often fall off or obstruct the players' vision.

In 1860, the Brooklyn Excelsiors baseball team started wearing a different type of hat, known as a "Brooklyn-style" cap. These caps were made of wool and had a round, flat crown with a short, stiff brim. The cap was designed to fit snugly on the head and could be worn backwards or forwards depending on the player's preference.

Over time, other baseball teams began to adopt similar caps, and by the late 19th century, baseball caps had become a standard part of the baseball uniform. The design of the caps continued to evolve, with different teams using different colors and materials to make their caps unique.

In the early 20th century, baseball caps started to become popular outside of the world of baseball. They were often worn by workers and farmers to protect their faces from the sun, and they became common pieces of headwear for outdoor activities like fishing and hunting.

During the 1920s and 1930s, baseball caps began to be used as a promotional item. Companies would print their logos on caps and give them away to advertise their products. This trend continued through the mid-20th century, and today, baseball caps are still a popular item for companies to use in their marketing efforts.

In the 1950s and 1960s, baseball caps became a fashion statement. They were worn by young people to express their individuality and to show support for their favorite sports teams. The popularity of baseball caps continued to grow in the following decades, with different styles and designs emerging to meet the demands of consumers.

One of the most iconic moments in the history of baseball caps came in the 1980s, when rap group Run-DMC began wearing New York Yankees caps as part of their signature style. This helped to popularize the trend of wearing caps with the brim facing forward, rather than backwards, and it cemented the cap's place as a fashion accessory.

Today, baseball caps are worn by people all over the world for a variety of reasons. They are still a standard part of the baseball uniform, and they are also used in other sports like golf and tennis. They are popular among people of all ages and genders, and they continue to be used to show support for sports teams, companies, and causes.

94 THE FLY SWATTER

The fly swatter is a simple yet effective tool that has been used for centuries to combat pesky flies and other flying insects. Its origins can be traced back to ancient times, where people used various means to rid themselves of insects. However, it was not until the late 19th century that the modern fly swatter, as we know it today, was invented.

The first documented use of a fly swatter can be found in ancient Egypt, where people used a variety of tools to swat flies and other insects. These included fans made of ostrich feathers, which were waved back and forth to create a breeze that would keep the insects at bay. Other materials used included palm fronds and strips of cloth.

In medieval Europe, people used a similar method to keep flies away. They would burn various herbs and plants, such as rosemary and lavender, to create a fragrant smoke that would repel insects. They also used fans made of feathers or cloth to create a breeze and keep the bugs from landing on them.

It wasn't until the late 19th century that the modern fly swatter was invented. In 1876, a woman named Alice H. Parker patented a fly trap that used a sticky substance to capture flies. However, this method was messy and not very effective.

In 1905, an inventor named Frank H. Rose created the first practical fly swatter. His design consisted of a wire handle with a flat, perforated metal or leather head that could be used to swat flies. The holes in the head allowed air to pass through, creating a loud noise that would startle the flies and make them easier to catch.

Rose's fly swatter was a huge success and soon became a household item. Other inventors soon followed suit, creating their own versions of the fly swatter. Some used rubber heads instead of metal or leather, while others added a plastic handle for better grip.

Over the years, the design of the fly swatter has evolved, but its basic principle remains the same. Today, you can find fly swatters in a variety of shapes and sizes, from the traditional flat-headed design to swatters shaped like tennis rackets.

Despite the many advances in pest control technology, the humble fly swatter remains a popular and effective tool for keeping flies and other flying insects at bay. Whether made of metal, leather, rubber, or plastic, the fly swatter is a timeless classic that has stood the test of time.

95 PORCELAIN DOLLS

Porcelain dolls are some of the most beloved and cherished toys in history. Their elegant beauty and intricate details have captured the imaginations of collectors and enthusiasts for centuries. The origins of porcelain dolls can be traced back to ancient civilizations, and their evolution has taken them through a fascinating journey over time.

The earliest recorded use of porcelain can be traced back to the Tang Dynasty in China (618-907 AD). Chinese artisans were the first to create porcelain dolls, which were crafted by molding a mixture of porcelain clay and water into shape and firing it in a kiln. The resulting doll was hard, smooth, and had a glossy finish. These dolls were often adorned with intricately painted costumes and accessories.

Porcelain dolls were first introduced to Europe during the 17th century. The first porcelain dolls were imported from China, and they were highly prized possessions of European aristocracy. These dolls were rare and expensive, and only the wealthiest individuals could afford them.

It was not until the 18th century that porcelain dolls began to be produced in Europe. The earliest known European porcelain dolls were made in Germany, and they were known as "bisque" dolls. These dolls were created using a mixture of porcelain, gypsum, and talc, which gave them a slightly different texture and appearance than the Chinese porcelain dolls.

The 19th century saw the rise of mass-produced porcelain dolls. French companies such as Jumeau, Bru, and Gaultier became famous for their high-quality porcelain dolls, which were produced in large quantities and exported all over the world. The dolls were typically dressed in the latest fashions of the time, and they became popular toys for children.

In the United States, porcelain dolls became popular during the Victorian era. These dolls were often used as decorations in the homes of wealthy families, and they were also given as gifts to children. American companies such as Kestner and Hertwig produced high-quality porcelain dolls that were highly sought after by collectors.

The 20th century saw a decline in the popularity of porcelain dolls, as new materials such as plastic and vinyl became more widely available. However, porcelain dolls continued to be produced and remain popular among collectors to this day.

Today, there are many different types of porcelain dolls, each with its unique history and style. Some of the most popular types of porcelain dolls include antique dolls, modern dolls, and artist dolls. Antique dolls are typically over 100 years old and are highly prized by collectors. Modern dolls are often produced in limited editions and are highly collectible. Artist dolls are one-of-a-kind creations that are crafted by individual artists and are highly sought after by collectors.

96 SUNSCREEN

Sunscreen has become an essential part of daily life, especially in hot and sunny climates. People apply it to protect their skin from harmful UV rays that can cause sunburn, skin cancer, and premature aging. However, the history of sunscreen dates back centuries, and it has evolved from a simple mix of natural ingredients to a scientifically formulated product.

Ancient civilizations, such as the Greeks and Egyptians, used a mix of olive oil and clay to protect their skin from the sun. In India, people applied sandalwood paste to their skin to block UV rays. Native Americans used a paste made of cornmeal, while the Chinese used rice bran oil. These natural ingredients were effective to some extent, but they were not standardized or tested for their sun protection factor (SPF).

In the 1930s, a Swiss chemistry student named Franz Greiter got a severe sunburn while climbing a mountain in the Swiss Alps. He realized that sunburn was not caused by heat but by UV radiation. He then developed a product called Gletscher Creme, which contained natural ingredients such as zinc oxide and cocoa butter. The cream was tested on volunteers and found to provide a measure of sun protection. Greiter later coined the term "sun protection factor" or SPF to describe the degree of protection provided by his product.

In the 1940s, during World War II, soldiers in the Pacific theater were issued a cream called "red vet pet" to protect their skin from the sun. The cream contained para-aminobenzoic acid (PABA), a chemical that absorbs UV radiation. PABA was later used in commercial sunscreens, but it was found to cause skin irritation and allergic reactions in some people.

In the 1960s, chemist Franz Greiter developed a new sunscreen formula that did not contain PABA. He called it "Piz Buin" after the mountain in Switzerland where he got sunburned. The formula contained a mix of chemical and physical blockers, including octyl methoxycinnamate, benzophenone 3, and titanium dioxide. Piz Buin became one of the first commercially available sunscreens with an SPF rating.

In the 1970s, the US Food and Drug Administration (FDA) began to regulate sunscreens, and manufacturers had to provide evidence of their products' efficacy. This led to the development of more effective and stable sunscreen ingredients, such as avobenzone, octocrylene, and oxybenzone.

In the 1980s, Australian researchers developed a new sunscreen formula that contained a combination of physical and chemical blockers. This sunscreen, known as "broad-spectrum" sunscreen, could block both UVB and UVA rays, which are responsible for skin cancer and premature aging, respectively. This was a significant breakthrough in sun protection technology, and it became the gold standard for modern sunscreens.

In the 1990s, the FDA approved the use of zinc oxide and titanium dioxide as physical blockers in sunscreens. These minerals are effective in blocking UV rays, but they were notorious for leaving a thick, white residue on the skin. However, advances in technology have enabled manufacturers to create micronized versions of these minerals, which are more transparent and cosmetically appealing.

In recent years, concerns have arisen about the safety of some sunscreen ingredients, such as oxybenzone and octinoxate. These chemicals are believed to be harmful to coral reefs and marine life, and some studies suggest that they may disrupt hormonal activity in humans. As a result, some countries, such as Hawaii and Palau, have banned the use of sunscreens containing these chemicals.

97 GARDEN RAKES

Garden rakes have been an essential tool for maintaining gardens and farms for thousands of years. The earliest known versions of rakes were made of wood and were used for gathering crops and clearing debris. Over time, the design and materials used to make garden rakes have evolved, and they have become an indispensable tool for any gardener.

The earliest evidence of the use of a rake dates back to around 2000 BCE in Ancient Egypt. These early rakes were made from reeds or papyrus and were used for clearing the ground before planting crops. Rakes were also used for collecting harvested crops, such as grains and fruits.

In ancient Greece, garden rakes were also used for collecting crops, and they were made of wood or bronze. Greek rakes were typically long handled and had a series of prongs or tines, like modern-day rakes.

In medieval Europe, rakes were an essential tool for maintaining the large gardens and farms of the aristocracy. They were typically made of wood or iron, and their design was like that of the Greek rakes. However, the European rakes often had longer handles and were sometimes decorated with intricate designs.

During the Renaissance, gardening became a popular hobby among the wealthy, and garden rakes became more elaborate and decorative. Rakes were often adorned with elaborate designs and made of expensive materials such as silver and gold.

In the 18th century, the industrial revolution brought about significant changes in the manufacturing of garden rakes. Rakes were now being mass-produced in factories, and the designs became more standardized. The introduction of new materials, such as steel, made rakes more durable and efficient.

During the 19th century, gardening became a popular pastime among the middle classes, and garden rakes became more affordable and widely available. Rakes were now made of materials such as wrought iron and bamboo.

In the 20th century, the development of new materials such as plastic and aluminum revolutionized the garden rake industry. These materials were lighter and more durable than traditional materials, and they made rakes more efficient and easier to use.

Today, garden rakes come in a variety of shapes, sizes, and materials, and they are an essential tool for maintaining gardens and farms. Some of the most popular types of rakes include leaf rakes, lawn rakes, and garden hoes.

Leaf rakes are used for collecting fallen leaves and other debris from lawns and gardens. They typically have long, flexible tines that are made of plastic or metal.

Lawn rakes are used for removing dead grass and other debris from lawns. They typically have short, rigid tines that are made of metal.

Garden hoes are used for cultivating soil and removing weeds. They typically have a long handle and a flat blade that is made of metal.

In addition to these traditional rakes, there are also a variety of specialized rakes available for specific gardening tasks, such as thatch rakes and bow rakes.

98 THE MINT JULEP

The mint julep is a classic Southern cocktail that is often associated with horse races, especially the Kentucky Derby. It is a refreshing and sweet drink that is traditionally made with bourbon, mint, sugar, and crushed ice. The origins of the mint julep can be traced back to the early 19th century, and its history is closely tied to the history of the South and its culture.

The word "julep" is believed to have been derived from the Arabic word "julab," which refers to a sweet, rose-flavored drink that was popular in the Middle East during the medieval period. The drink was introduced to Europe by the Moors, and it eventually made its way to the New World with the early colonists.

The first written record of the mint julep dates to the early 1800s. At that time, the drink was primarily made with brandy or rum, as these spirits were more readily available in the South than bourbon. The recipe for the mint julep was also different than the one used today, as it called for sugar and water to be mixed with the alcohol, rather than just sugar.

Over time, the recipe for the mint julep evolved to include bourbon, which became more widely available in the South in the mid-19th century. The use of bourbon in the drink is often attributed to a Kentucky senator named Henry Clay, who is said to have introduced the drink to Washington, D.C. in the 1850s.

The popularity of the mint julep continued to grow in the South throughout the 19th century. It became a popular drink at social gatherings and was often served at weddings, garden parties, and other outdoor events.

The drink was also closely associated with the Kentucky Derby, which began in 1875. The mint julep became the official drink of the Kentucky Derby in 1938, and it has been a staple of the event ever since.

The mint julep has also been immortalized in literature and film. It was a favorite drink of the character Scarlett O'Hara in Margaret Mitchell's novel "Gone with the Wind," and it has appeared in numerous movies and TV shows set in the South. The drink is also referenced in many popular songs, including "Mint Julep" by Louis Armstrong and "Mint Juleps and Needles" by Duke Ellington.

Today, the mint julep remains a beloved drink in the South and beyond. Its popularity has spread throughout the country, and it is now a common drink at bars and restaurants across the United States. Many variations of the drink have also emerged over the years, including versions made with different types of alcohol, such as gin or tequila.

Despite its evolution over time, the mint julep remains a quintessential Southern drink with a rich history and cultural significance. Its association with the Kentucky Derby has helped to cement its place in American culture, and it's refreshing taste and simple recipe continue to make it a favorite drink for all occasions.

99 PICKLES

Pickles are a type of preserved food that have been enjoyed by people all over the world for thousands of years. The history of pickles spans cultures and continents, and it provides us with a window into the evolution of human civilization.

The origin of pickles can be traced back to ancient Mesopotamia, where people began to preserve cucumbers in brine around 2400 BC. Pickles were valued for their ability to last for long periods of time without spoiling, which made them a valuable source of food during times of scarcity. In fact, pickles were so highly prized in ancient times that they were often used as a form of currency, and they were even buried with the dead as a form of sustenance in the afterlife.

From Mesopotamia, the art of pickling spread to other parts of the world, including India, where pickles made from mangoes, lemons, and other fruits and vegetables became a popular accompaniment to meals. In ancient Egypt, pickled vegetables such as cucumbers and onions were also a staple food, and they were often served alongside bread and beer.

Pickles became an important part of European cuisine during the Middle Ages, when they were used to preserve food during the long winter months. The word "pickle" is thought to have come from the Dutch word "pekel," which means "brine." In England, pickled vegetables such as onions and cucumbers were often served as a side dish, and pickled herring was a popular snack.

During the Age of Exploration, pickles became an important food for sailors, who would often suffer from scurvy during long voyages. Pickled vegetables, especially cucumbers, were a good source of vitamin C, which helped to prevent scurvy. The use of pickles on ships also led to the development of a new type of pickle, the gherkin, which is a small, tart pickle made from a specific type of cucumber.

In America, pickles have a long and storied history. The first recorded pickle factory in the United States was established in 1820 by William Underwood in Boston, Massachusetts. Underwood's pickles became so popular that he soon had to move his factory to a larger location. During the Civil War, pickles became an important source of food for soldiers, and they were often included in their rations.

In the late 19th and early 20th centuries, pickles became a popular snack food in America, and many different types of pickles were developed, including dill pickles, bread and butter pickles, and sweet pickles. In the 1920s and 1930s, pickles were even used as a marketing tool, with companies like Vlasic using catchy slogans like "the pickle that tickles" to sell their products.

Today, pickles continue to be a popular food all over the world. In addition to cucumbers, pickles can be made from a wide variety of fruits and vegetables, including beets, carrots, and even watermelon rind. Pickles are also used in a variety of dishes, including sandwiches, salads, and soups.

In addition to their culinary uses, pickles have also played a role in medicine and folklore. In traditional medicine, pickles have been used to treat a variety of ailments, including indigestion and sore throats. In folklore, pickles have been associated with luck and fertility, and they have been used in various rituals and ceremonies.

100 THE TOOTHBRUSH

The toothbrush is an essential tool for maintaining dental hygiene, and it has undergone significant changes throughout history. The toothbrush, as we know it today, has an interesting history, dating back to ancient civilizations.

The ancient Egyptians were the first to use a form of the toothbrush. They would chew on small twigs with frayed ends to clean their teeth. In other parts of the world, people used a variety of tools to clean their teeth, such as the chew sticks made from twigs, or the porcupine quills used by Native Americans.

The first toothbrush with bristles that resembled modern-day toothbrushes was invented in China in the 15th century. The Chinese toothbrush had a handle made from bamboo or animal bone and bristles made from the hair of pigs, horses, or badgers. It was not until the 17th century that toothbrushes began to appear in Europe. Wealthy Europeans used toothbrushes made from ivory or bone handles with boar bristles.

In the late 1700s, William Addis, an Englishman, was credited with inventing the modern-day toothbrush. While in prison, Addis drilled holes into a cattle bone and inserted boar bristles to make a handle. After his release, he started a business manufacturing toothbrushes. By the early 19th century, the toothbrush had become popular in Europe and was being mass-produced.

In America, the first toothbrush was invented in 1780 by William Kent. He used animal bristles and attached them to a piece of carved bone. The first mass-produced toothbrush in the United States was made in 1885 by

H.N. Wadsworth. It had a bone handle and bristles made from the hair of Siberian hogs.

In 1938, Dupont de Nemours introduced nylon bristles. Nylon was a more durable material than animal hair and did not harbor bacteria as easily. Nylon bristles quickly became the standard for toothbrushes and are still used today.

In the 1960s, the first electric toothbrush was developed in Switzerland. It was called the Broxodent and was not very popular at first because of its high cost. However, as prices came down, electric toothbrushes became more common. Today, electric toothbrushes are a popular option for people who want a more thorough clean.

Toothbrushes have come a long way since their invention. They are now available in a variety of shapes, sizes, and materials. Some toothbrushes have angled bristles to reach difficult areas, while others have soft bristles for sensitive teeth. There are even toothbrushes with Bluetooth connectivity that can sync with a phone app to track brushing habits.

In addition to the toothbrush, toothpaste has also undergone significant changes. The ancient Egyptians used a mixture of crushed eggshells, myrrh, and pumice to clean their teeth. In the early 19th century, toothpaste was sold as powder, and people would sprinkle it on their toothbrushes. Today, toothpaste is available in a variety of flavors and is formulated to fight tooth decay, gum disease, and bad breath.

101 THE BUTTON

The button, a small and simple device used to fasten clothing, has a history that dates to ancient times. Over the centuries, the button has evolved from a purely functional item to a decorative and fashionable accessory and has played an important role in the development of modern fashion and clothing design.

The earliest buttons can be traced back to ancient civilizations such as the Egyptians and the Indus Valley civilization, where they were made from materials like bone, ivory, and shell. These buttons were often used for ornamental purposes and were sewn onto clothing to add embellishment and decoration.

It wasn't until the 13th century that buttons began to be used as fasteners for clothing. At this time, buttons were made from a variety of materials, including wood, metal, and bone, and were often used on garments like jackets and tunics. In medieval Europe, buttons were also used on religious garments like cassocks and vestments and were sometimes made from precious metals and gemstones.

By the 16th century, buttons had become an essential part of men's clothing, particularly for soldiers and other military personnel. Buttons were used on jackets, waistcoats, and breeches, and were often made from metal or horn. During this time, buttons also began to be used on women's clothing, particularly on corsets and bodices.

In the 17th and 18th centuries, buttons continued to be an important part of men's clothing, particularly for the wealthy and aristocratic classes. Buttons made from gold, silver, and other precious metals were popular, as were buttons featuring intricate designs and engravings. Women's clothing also began to feature more elaborate button designs during this time, particularly on dresses and gowns.

In the 19th century, the Industrial Revolution brought about significant changes in the way buttons were produced. Machines were invented that could mass-produce buttons, making them more affordable and accessible to the general public. Buttons made from a variety of materials, including wood, bone, and mother-of-pearl, were widely available, and the use of buttons on clothing became even more widespread.

During the 20th century, buttons continued to play an important role in fashion and clothing design. In the early part of the century, buttons made from plastics like celluloid and Bakelite became popular and were often used on clothing and accessories like purses and hats. In the 1960s and 70s, buttons made from natural materials like wood, bone, and horn enjoyed a resurgence in popularity, particularly in the realm of hippie fashion.

Today, buttons continue to be an essential part of clothing design and are used in a wide variety of styles and materials. From functional plastic buttons used on everyday clothing, to decorative buttons made from precious metals and gemstones, the humble button has come a long way from its ancient origins.

In addition to their functional and decorative uses, buttons have also played an important role in culture and symbolism throughout history. In many cultures, buttons have been used to signify status and rank, particularly in military and governmental organizations. Buttons have also been used as political symbols, particularly during times of social upheaval and unrest.

102 THE ZIPPER

The zipper, also known as the zip, is a popular device used for fastening clothes and other textile products. It has revolutionized the fashion industry and made life easier for people around the world. The invention of the zipper has a history that spans over a century.

The first known design for a zipper-like fastener was created by Elias Howe, the inventor of the sewing machine, in 1851. He called it the "Automatic Continuous Clothing Closure," and it was intended to be used for shoes. However, he did not pursue the invention and instead focused on his sewing machine.

It wasn't until the late 1800s that the idea of a zipper resurfaced. In 1891, Whitcomb L. Judson, an American inventor from Chicago, invented a device that he called the "Clasp Locker." It was made of hooks and eyes that were attached to a sliding metal frame, which could be opened and closed. The device was marketed as a fastener for shoes, but it was not successful, as it was difficult to use and often broke.

In 1906, Swedish-American inventor Gideon Sundback began working on a new design for a fastener that would be more reliable and easier to use. He developed a system of interlocking teeth that could be opened and closed using a slider. Sundback patented his design in 1917, and the following year, he sold the rights to the B.F. Goodrich Company.

The B.F. Goodrich Company first used Sundback's design on rubber boots and then on galoshes. They called the device the "zipper" because of the sound it made when it was opened and closed. However, the zipper did not catch on as a clothing fastener until the 1920s.

In 1923, the zipper was first used in men's trousers. The fashion industry was initially skeptical of the new fastener, and it took several years for it to gain widespread acceptance. However, by the 1930s, zippers were commonly used in women's dresses, and they had become a symbol of modernity and convenience.

During World War II, zippers were used extensively in military uniforms and equipment, which helped to increase their popularity even further. After the war, zippers were used in a wide variety of products, from luggage and handbags to furniture and automobiles.

In the 1950s, zippers began to be used in jeans, which helped to solidify their place as a staple of casual fashion. In the 1960s, zippers became a popular decorative element in clothing, and they were often used to add a touch of edginess to an outfit.

In the 1970s, the fashion industry began to experiment with new materials and designs for zippers. Nylon zippers became popular, as they were lightweight and durable. Zippers were also used in more creative ways, such as on the sides of clothing, to add ventilation or adjustability.

Today, zippers are used in a wide variety of products, from clothing and accessories to sports equipment and industrial machinery. They are available in many different materials, colors, and designs, and they continue to be a popular and versatile fastener.

103 THE PAPERCLIP

The paperclip is a humble office tool that has been a staple of desk drawers for over a century. While it may seem like a simple object, the paperclip has a history that spans continents and involves inventors, designers, and businesspeople.

The origins of the paperclip are shrouded in mystery, as there are multiple claims to its invention. One of the earliest known patents for a paperclip was filed in 1867 by Samuel B. Fay, an American inventor. Fay's paperclip was like the modern paperclip in shape and function and was designed to hold papers together without damaging them. However, Fay's design was not widely adopted and remained relatively unknown.

The paperclip gained widespread popularity in Europe in the late 19th and early 20th centuries. In 1899, a Norwegian inventor named Johan Vaaler patented a paperclip design that featured a triangular shape with two round loops at the ends. Vaaler's design was not initially successful, but it gained popularity in Norway during World War II when other types of fasteners were difficult to come by.

Another early paperclip design was created by a British engineer named Gem. In 1901, Gem patented a paperclip that was made from a single piece of wire bent into a simple, double-looped shape. Gem's paperclip design became very popular in the United Kingdom and is still in use today.

In the United States, the most widely recognized paperclip design is the "Gem" clip, which was introduced in 1892 by the Gem Manufacturing Company. The Gem clip was similar in shape to the paperclip designed by

Gem in Britain, but it was made from a thinner wire and had a smoother surface. The Gem clip quickly became popular in the US and remains one of the most common paperclip designs in use today.

During World War II, the paperclip took on a new importance as a symbol of resistance against the Nazi regime. Norwegians wore paperclips on their lapels as a sign of solidarity with the Jews and other victims of Nazi persecution. The paperclip became known as a symbol of Norwegian resistance to oppression and is still used as a symbol of peace and unity today.

In the decades since World War II, the paperclip has remained a regular office tool. While the basic design has remained largely unchanged, there have been countless variations and improvements on the original concept. Some paper clips are made from plastic or other materials, while others are coated in colors or patterns to make them more visually appealing.

Today, the paperclip is still an important part of office culture around the world. Despite the rise of digital technology, paper documents are still an essential part of many businesses, and the paperclip remains a vital tool for keeping those documents organized. From its humble beginnings as a simple wire fastener, the paperclip has become an enduring symbol of efficiency, organization, and creativity.

ABOUT THE AUTHOR

Keb Pound was born, raised, and lives in Jacksonville, Florida with his "Soon-to-be-World-Famous-Wife" and two children.

Keb has performed Stand-up comedy, been a "On Air" radio personality on a local Jacksonville Sports Talk radio station, and hosted multiple podcasts including "UNFILTERED", "REFILTERED", and the most bingeable podcast in the world, "The Stupid History Minute".

Keb enjoys a nice glass of Jack Daniel's, the Florida Gators, the Jacksonville Jaguars, and of course, the Atlanta Braves.

Made in the USA
Columbia, SC
21 September 2023

23110908R00117